An International Center for Learning
Christian Education/Christian School

How To Do
BIBLE LEARNING ACTIVITIES

GRADES 7-12

Compiled by Rich Bundschuh
and Annette Parrish

Illustrated by Rick Bundschuh

INTERNATIONAL CENTER FOR LEARNING
A Subsidiary of GL Publications, Ventura, California, U.S.A.

Acknowledgments
Contributing Writers

Jim Dahl

Jarol Duerksen

Annette Parrish

Rick Bundschuh

Sherie Lindvall

Ed Stewart

Monroe Marlowe

Marian Wiggins

Dr. Neal McBride

Unless otherwise noted, Scripture quotations are from *The New International Version. Holy Bible.* Copyright 1978 by New York International Bible Society. Used by permission.

Published by International Center for Learning
GL Publications, Ventura, California 93006.
Printed in U.S.A.

ISBN 0-8307-0917-7

WHERE TO FIND . . .

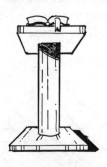

UNDERSTANDING AND USING BIBLE LEARNING ACTIVITIES (BLA's)

This chapter will help you to:
1. Explain what Bible learning activities are and why they are important
2. Describe the ABC lesson development
3. Summarize the idea and use of early arrival/fellowship activities
4. List and gather the basic supplies needed to effectively use BLA's.

GENERAL GUIDELINES

Understanding BLA's

Do the young people in your Sunday School class have the blahs? If you take their blahs and get rid of the "h" (hassle, hodgepodge, hollowness, humdrum, hectic, etc.), what you have left are the BLA's (Bible Learning Activities).

BLA's are the various methods by which a creative teacher involves his or her class members in the first-hand discovery of biblical truth. Let's look a bit closer at the phrase, "Bible learning activity." Moving backwards, the third word ACTIVITY suggests that we want our learners to be active participants in the learning process, not merely passive observers. Meaningless "fun and games," activity for activity's sake, or a group "pooling of ignorance" is not the idea. The object is to select BLA's that directly contribute to the accomplishment of specific learning objectives.

LEARNING indicates that the purpose of the activity is to promote change in the learners. Learning is change; a change in knowledge (facts, information), attitudes (feeling, opinion), and/or behavior (skill, ability). Our task as teachers is to help teenagers change and become more like Jesus Christ. Therefore, a BLA should facilitate learning that leads toward this change process.

Lastly, a BLA is a learning activity that is centered in the BIBLE. God's Word is our standard for both faith and practice. Consequently, a Bible learning activity is a task or method that is centered in helping our students to gain God's perspective as revealed in the Bible.

The Benefit of BLA's

Young people learn best when they are actively involved in the teaching/learning process. According to studies on learning, students who merely "sit and listen" retain significantly less content than those who are personally involved in well-planned learning activities. Students retain 90 percent, after three days, of what they hear, see, and do. Conversely, they retain only 10 percent of what they hear. The point is clear, the more a student is involved the more he/she will learn.

BLA's are merely the methods you provide your class members so that they can "help themselves" to learn spiritual truth. The premise is, don't tell a student something that he can discover for himself. BLA's assist the student to do this very thing. As a result, while simple telling may pass on information, planned involvement leads not only to information but to superior and lasting learning in the largest sense of the idea.

Tips for Guiding Group/Individual Involvement

Proper use of BLA's is very important. Here are some useful tips that have proven to be valuable:

1. How to start Gradually introduce involvement to your class. Begin with low-threat activities. For example:

- Use an involvement activity at the beginning of the hour (the Approach section of the ABC plan outlined on page 8), but use a familiar teaching style for the rest of the hour.
- When people are comfortable with this, use some involvement learning during Conclusion/Decision (at the end of the hour).
- Replace the "opening exercise" with a Fellowship activity.
- Begin using Bible learning activities during Bible Exploration. Start with a low-threat activity such as a neighbor-nudge (two people briefly talk over an assigned topic or question).

2. Clear instructions Whether you are teaching one person or a group of 30 learners, the necessity of clear, simple instructions cannot be overstressed. Verbal instructions should always be accompanied by some type of written instructions. Writing the instructions on the chalkboard, a poster, the overhead, on small index cards, or any other method will help assure that your learners understand what you are asking them to do. Making instructions clear and to the point will make the task easier and more productive for the learners.

3. Leader and recorder When using BLA's that call for small groups (4 to 7 persons), make sure the groups appoint a leader and a recorder. The leader serves to keep the group on track while the recorder takes notes or in some other manner records the group's results. You may need to provide some direction by stating, for example, "The person wearing the most blue will be your leader, and the person who lives the farthest away should be your recorder."

4. Time limits Always state the amount of time the group(s) will have to complete the task. Group members will be more motivated to work if they know there is a time limit. Once or twice during the activity tell them how much time they have left. Learners will often do as much work in the last three minutes of a ten-minute project as they did in the first seven minutes. Remember, time limits are flexible; feel free to add or subtract time as the abilities and interests of your class may necessitate.

5. Encourage students Assure your students that you have confidence in their ability to accomplish the learning activity. By being alert to your students' "comfort level" and selecting activities which you are fairly certain they can handle, your encouragement will be well founded. Telling them you are available for questions and further explanation will also serve to encourage their efforts.

6. Let them do it! You may know all the answers and may know the best way to complete the task you have assigned, but let your class members find the answers for themselves and do the project with their own minds and hands. Guide them, encourage them, assist them, but let them do it.

7. Needed resources Make certain that you have on hand an ample supply of those materials necessary to complete the activity. Nothing can be more frustrating for your students than not having what they need to finish the task.

8. Reporting results How will you have the individuals or groups report the results of their efforts? Students enjoy hearing or seeing what others have done. In large groups you may ask for a few volunteers to share, or have each group share one idea each before opening it up to further suggestions or comments. Art projects can be affixed to the wall or placed on a bulletin board. Creative songs that apply biblical truth can be sung. The principle is to allow students to benefit from mutual sharing of ideas and results.

9. Be appreciative Thank students for their effort whether they complete their project or not. Every word of appreciation and affirmation is an investment in the future of your class as an involvement-oriented learning experience.

Asking the Right Questions

Fortunately the creative teacher does not have to be skilled in all the arts of group dynamics in order to use BLA's successfully. But learning how to use questions as a teaching tool can be of tremendous value to a teacher. Well-thought-out questions will help learners to identify and evaluate information, to interpret it, and to assess how that information affects their values and decision making. This means you must choose your questions with care. Here are six suggestions that will help you in choosing good questions:

1. Questions should require the learner to think. Avoid asking questions which may be answered with only yes or no.

2. Keep the questions brief and simple, restricting each question to only one main thought. Often we confuse our students by actually asking several questions within one question. Make certain your questions are clearly focused.

3. Distinguish between a question asking for facts and one seeking feelings or opinions.

4. Avoid asking questions which the group cannot answer because of a lack of information or background. Also, stay away from highly personal questions as discussion starters. Many a group discussion has failed to get off the ground because a well-meaning teacher began with a question that learners were afraid to answer.

5. The questions should be a natural part of the class session, not something artificially tacked on at the end to fill some time.

6. The tone and manner of your questions should encourage the learners to express themselves. A friendly, pleasant and sincere tone of voice will encourage confidence and understanding. Remember, while every contribution may not be worthwhile, every *contributor* is!

Keeping in mind these basic suggestions for good questioning, let's examine three different types of questions that you can use:

Informational Questions An informational question requires the learner to remember or refer to specific facts in order to answer the question correctly. A teacher can discern how well a learner knows the basic facts or guide the discovery of those facts by the proper use of an informational question.

Examples: Where was Jesus born? According to Matthew 20:21, what was Jesus' answer to the rich young man? What was the name of the river in which Jesus was baptized?

It is almost impossible to have a meaningful discussion guided by informational questions alone. Therefore, we also need analytical questions.

Analytical Questions Analytical questions encourage learners to attach meaning or explore principles in facts. Questions of this type are more open-ended than informational questions. By using this type of question the teacher helps learners share what they understand and perceive about the facts.

Examples: What do you think Jesus had in mind when He said . . . ? How do you think Jesus felt when He was being questioned by Pilate? What are some possible reasons that caused Peter to deny Jesus three times?

Personal Questions Personal questions seek to draw personal application of facts, draw out a learner's values, and explore attitudes. Questions on this level are effective means for engaging learners in the process of reflecting, expressing and acting on concerns that relate to them personally. The focus of these questions is to guide learners in their own decision making and value forming.

Examples: If you had been an apostle what would you have done when Jesus was arrested? How does your life reflect the model we have in Jesus Christ? What is your idea of being "Christlike"?

ABC LESSON DEVELOPMENT

Bible learning activities are appropriate for all three sections of the ABC lesson format. To illustrate, three examples are presented below for each of the three session parts—Approach to the Word, Bible Exploration, and Conclusion and Decision.

Approach to the Word

Each session should begin with a learning activity designed to capture the interest of your class and introduce the theme of the session. The idea is to whet their appetites for the Bible study that follows. Here are three Approach ideas that could be used with a lesson on the Old Testament figure Elijah taken from I Kings 19:

1. Tape a length of butcher paper to the chalkboard and divide it into three sections. Divide the class into three groups and have group one define fear and write their definition in section one. Have the second group list things that make today's Christians afraid. In the third section have the third group list things people do when they are afraid.

2. Present the following situation to students: You are rappelling. You make a wrong move and find yourself dangling by a rope off the edge of a cliff. From somewhere you hear a voice cry, "If you let go I'll catch you!" but you cannot see who said it or where the person is. Now ask students what they would feel in this situation and what they would be thinking. What would help them trust the voice? What would make that difficult?

3. Ask each student to think of one time he/she was really afraid. Have students tell a neighbor how they felt and what they did in that circumstance.

Bible Exploration

The Bible Exploration is the heart of your class session because it involves each learner directly in the study of God's Word. It is during this portion of the session that you have your learners, through the Exploration activity that you choose to use, explore and discover what the Bible says and means, and discuss its implications for life today. A wide variety of methods is possible. Using the same passage we used in the previous section on the Approach to the Word, here are three possible Bible Exploration activities:

1. Have groups read the passage and make a collage depicting the events in the life of Elijah as found in that chapter.

8

2. Using a tape recorder, have the students play the characters involved and record a radio interview that focuses on the events, attitudes, and feelings potentially experienced by the characters.

3. Prepare a series of 5 to 10 questions that can facilitate a discussion on the passage. Guide students to talk about their feelings and fears that may be similar to those experienced by Elijah.

Conclusion and Decision

After having spent the majority of the class time discussing what God's Word says and means, each learner needs to apply the truths of Scripture to his or her own life. Questions such as, "What is Scripture asking of me?" or "How can I put it into practice in my own life?" are the main thrust of this section of the lesson plan. The Conclusion and Decision activity may be so personal in nature that you will not want to ask your students to share with each other. Other times, however, it will be very appropriate to gather in small groups and report how the Scriptures previously studied apply to their personal relationships to God and others. Here are three possible Conclusion and Decision activities:

1. Have students select a prayer partner and pray for each other in light of the biblical truth studied.

2. Write the following statement on the board, "Lord, it seems to me you do expect too much of me sometimes, but I'm willing to try again in regards to . . . " Have each student complete the sentence by writing his/her answer on a piece of paper. Close the session with a time of silent prayer giving students the opportunity to bring their response before God.

3. Ask students to suggest ways that they, with God's help, can help one another handle fear and discouragement. List suggestions on the board (or overhead) as they are given. Ask each student to select one thing to do next week in this area for someone else. Close in prayer, asking for the strength and willingness to do that one thing.

Choosing/Evaluating the Best Method

What method is best for each part of the ABC lesson plan? The answer to this question is hard because most BLA's can be used in a variety of ways for each part of the lesson. For example, consider how "writing a prayer" could be used:

For the Approach: The leader begins by telling a story. "A Christian teenager has been ordered by his school principal to stop sharing his faith on campus. After leaving the principal's office, the student stops to pray." Write what you think you would pray in that situation. Allow time for writing, then guide the learners into the lesson.

For the Bible Exploration: After reading Acts 3:1-11, write a prayer the healed man might have prayed after entering the Temple. Write a prayer of thanks from a person who has just received Christ as Saviour.

For the Conclusion and Decision: Write a short prayer to God, asking for specific help with a specific problem that you are willing to commit to Him this week.

When selecting any method, remember that your choice should be based on:
1. the object or purpose of the session
2. the length of time available
3. the needs and interests of your class members
4. an understanding of how people learn

5. the equipment and facilities available

6. your own ability to use a particular method.

Remember, in selecting a BLA, variety and selectivity are keys. Stay away from using the same methods week after week. We all know that variety is the spice of life. This is also a big key in maintaining the interest of your students. Also, select BLA's that are appropriate for the content they are to be used with. Ask yourself the question, "Will this method accurately communicate the truth I want my students to gain?" If yes, use it; if not, select another.

Here is a list of additional criteria by which you can evaluate the Bible learning activities you are considering for any session. If the methods you select do not seem appropriate, adapt them or change them until they meet the learning objectives you have outlined.

1. The method should help direct attention to the specific nature of the learning task so that the learner will know what is expected. Is the learner expected to discuss, ask questions, give opinions or write? Clearly state what you expect each person to do.

2. A method should arouse interest and motivate the individual to want to learn about the subject being presented. Does the method put class members to sleep or make them sit up and say, "I want to know more about what you just said"?

3. A method should also be able to maintain interest. When more of the senses (hearing, seeing, etc.) are involved, interest will be greater.

4. A good teaching method avoids causing excessive frustration or failure on the part of the learner. Any method that continuously frustrates or does not allow success is not effective. Do your learners understand the terms you use? Are your visuals clear and accurate? Are your instructions clear? Are you asking people to do something they will feel comfortable about?

5. A teaching method should help the person transfer what has been learned to everyday life outside of class.

6. A method should help develop and maintain positive attitudes toward the teacher, the subject being taught and toward the learner himself/herself.

7. A method should fit the time limits in which it must fit and be appropriate to the section purpose of the ABC lesson plan.

EARLY ARRIVALS/FELLOWSHIP

The Bible learning activities spoken of thus far and presented in this book are mainly designed to be used within the ABC lesson format, or, in general, within your class period. So, what are you to do with early arrivals? One suitable answer to this question is to plan an informal activity that students can become involved in until it is time for class to begin. But more than just a time filler, this "early arrival activity" can be an effective tool in building an atmosphere of warmth and acceptance among your students that is so vital to group learning experiences. It is an opportunity to help your students get to know and appreciate each other and to establish lines of communication.

This is also a good time to make a point of greeting visitors. Prior to the activity, select two or three individuals who are responsible to greet newcomers and make them feel welcome. It is a good idea to have name tags available each week for all your class members. When everyone is wearing a name tag, visitors feel more comfortable and even "old timers" will appreciate the help name tags provide.

The following activities are a few examples of early arrival activities that are designed to encourage nonthreatening openness among class members. Select or adapt one of these activities to precede each of your class sessions. Provide some type of refreshment if it is appropriate for your class, but be sure to have an activity prepared to stimulate meaningful sharing. Not only will this actively involve your early arrivers, but it will likely make your other class members want to arrive on time.

The Title Is Me: Write on the chalkboard, flipchart or overhead transparency approximately 10 best-selling book titles or current film titles. Have each person study the list and select a title which says something about the past week he has experienced. Ask volunteers to share their title and a sentence of explanation with the class.

Meaningful Scriptures: Have volunteers share with the class a verse from the Bible which has been particularly meaningful to them within the last month. Be sure to have each person explain why the verses were meaningful.

Why Come? Have class members circulate in the group, answering the question, "Why do you attend this Bible class?"

Ideal Vacation: Give each person a sheet of paper on which to draw some symbol that represents his or her ideal vacation. Have people share these in groups of four, or display them on the bulletin board for all to see.

Task-Oriented Name Tags: Provide colored paper, scissors, felt pens and pins. Ask each person to select a color of paper and cut it into a shape which represents a major task in life (for a fireman, a fire hat; for a homemaker, a rolling pin; etc.). Then have each person write his or her name on the cutout and pin it to his clothing. Allow time for people to discuss briefly their task with others at random.

I'm Lonely: Have students gather in clusters of three or four and share one experience when they were lonely and how they handled it.

Life Goals: Have class members gather in small groups and share one life goal with each other. If time permits, have them talk about how they hope to accomplish that goal.

Personal Church History: Give each person a sheet of paper on which to complete this brief questionnaire.

1. When did you first attend this church (or group)?
2. What person(s) was most responsible for your attendance?
3. What was your first impression of the people?

Have people gather in clusters of three or four and share answers with one another.

Instant Inheritance: Have class members jot down their answers to the following question on a small index card and share it with others in groups of three: "If I could wish my children anything at all for an inheritance, what three things would I wish for them?"

I'm Thankful: Write the following incomplete statement on the chalkboard, flipchart or overhead transparency: "Today I'm thankful for . . . " Ask class members to think for one minute about how they would finish that statement. Then have people gather in clusters of three or four and share their answers.

Name, Rank and Cereal Number: As class members arrive ask them to form pairs and share their full name, the state or country of birth, and their favorite food.

Home Sweet Home: Have students share with two other individuals what city they consider to be their "hometown" and how long it has been since they last visited it.

R and R: Write the following statement on the chalkboard or overhead transparency: "Where is your favorite vacation spot and when were you there last?" Ask adults to form groups of three and share their answers with each other.

A Few of My Favorite Things: Distribute plain sheets of paper to students as they arrive. Instruct students to number from one to five and make a list of the things in life that they love to do. Have them specify which things they would not have listed five years ago. Encourage students to compare lists with at least one other person during the fellowship time.

Fantasy Island: As students enter the classroom, have them respond in pairs or triads to this statement, "If money were no object, I would like to visit (name of country) for one month. The first thing I would do is _____." Have statement written on chalkboard or overhead.

So Far So Good: Have class members share with one another the most meaningful thing they have learned so far in their study of the course. After five minutes, ask for several volunteers to share their responses.

In Living Color: Ask students to form groups of three and share their favorite colors and why they like those colors. Then ask them to recall what colors are mentioned in the Bible.

May Flowers? Distribute plain sheets of colored paper and ask students to tear a shape that represents what they like about the current month. Have each student share their paper tear with at least two other people.

A Little Dab'll Do Ya: Before class members arrive, write the following instructions: "Form pairs and discuss and defend your way of applying toothpaste to your toothbrush. Now find one person who shares your method and one who does not."

Tennis Anyone? As students arrive, have them neighbor-nudge about the last competitive sports event in which they participated or paid to see; which sports they enjoy; and/or which sports they least enjoy.

Birthday Buddies: As students arrive, ask them to find the person in the class who has the birthday closest to theirs. Then have them share with each other their most special birthday.

They're Playing My Song: Ask class members to think of a song whose title or lyrics capture the quality of their recent week, or deal with something they have been thinking about all week. Ask people to share their song titles or lyrics with at least one other person during the fellowship time.

MATERIALS AND EQUIPMENT

To use BLA's effectively, you will need to collect and have on hand a number of different materials and equipment. Here is a checklist to help you. For every item you cannot check off, make creative plans for improvement.

Your classroom should possess the following characteristics to be appropriate for learning activities:
- [ ] 10 square feet minimum for each student
- [ ] Adequate lighting
- [ ] Proper ventilation
- [ ] Heating and cooling systems are functioning
- [ ] Acoustics are good

- ☐ Can be darkened enough for films or slides
- ☐ Electrical outlets are accessible
- ☐ Comfortable chairs, preferably ones which can be moved
- ☐ Tables to work at (or just sit around)
- ☐ Chalkboard, chalk, and eraser
- ☐ At least one bulletin board
- ☐ A screen or light-colored blank wall for projection

A supply of these items should be in the classroom at all times:

- ☐ Chalk
- ☐ Pencils or pens
- ☐ Felt marking pens
- ☐ Writing paper
- ☐ Drawing paper
- ☐ Masking tape
- ☐ Scissors
- ☐ Glue
- ☐ Newsprint tablet or roll of shelf or butcher paper
- ☐ Some discarded pictorial magazines
- ☐ Index cards
- ☐ A ball of string
- ☐ Paper clips

The following resource items should be available in the classroom for in-class use and check out:

- ☐ Extra Bibles, various versions
- ☐ Concordances
- ☐ Bible dictionary
- ☐ English dictionary
- ☐ Bible atlas
- ☐ Bible handbook
- ☐ Assorted Bible commentaries
- ☐ Christian books and periodicals

The following equipment may be available (shared with other classes) for optional use:

- ☐ Overhead projector
- ☐ Slide projector
- ☐ Filmstrip projector
- ☐ Motion picture projector
- ☐ Tape recorder
- ☐ Video tape recorder
- ☐ Personal computer
- ☐ Record player

Gathering Materials

As for gathering materials, here's a helpful tip: Leaf through your teacher's manual and make a shopping list from the "Materials Needed" section and the "Session Preparation" list that is usually included with each session plan. Take a couple of hours to gather the supplies you will need for the next few weeks or an entire quarter and store them in the classroom or at home for ready use. Check with your superintendent—perhaps your expenses may be reimbursed through the Sunday School or Christian education budget.

SELECTION CODES

You are now ready to begin using the various BLA suggestions presented in this book. To help you in your selection, a coding system has been used after the name of each activity. Each BLA is coded in two ways to help a teacher in selecting an activity.

1. The shaded part(s) of the arrow = the section(s) of a lesson which are most appropriate for that BLA. (A = Approach to the Word; B = Bible Exploration; C = Conclusion and Decision.)

2. The placement of the arrow designates the age level for which the BLA is most appropriate. For example, an arrow above the left half of the age-level bar designates an activity that is most appropriate for junior high students. An arrow at the middle of the bar designates an activity that is appropriate for both junior and senior high. An arrow above the right half of the bar designates an activity that is best for senior high students.

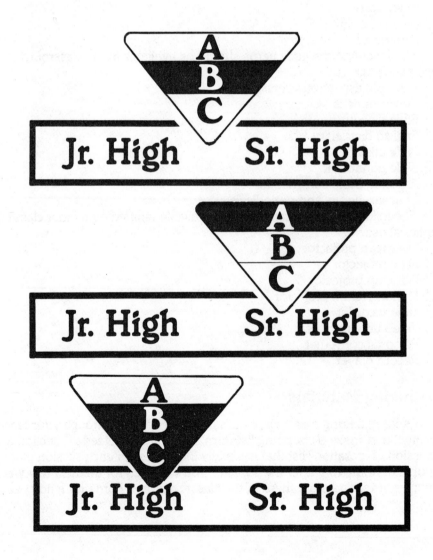

THE SIGHTS AND SOUNDS OF BIBLE LEARNING

Audiovisual Aids Which Can Help Your Lessons Live!

Audiovisual aids are vehicles which help the teacher convey the intangible truth of God to the immaterial hearts of the learners through the gateway of the physical senses (seeing, hearing, feeling, tasting, smelling). What we see, hear and touch during a Bible study session can make a difference in how effectively God's Word enters our hearts. The more we see, hear and touch—and the more we do these simultaneously—the more we learn. Though not as widely employed as the first three, the senses of taste and smell can also contribute to a positive learning experience (a fresh-smelling, fragrant classroom and occasional refreshments for the learners).

Many audiovisual tools have been present in the church for decades. But recent technological advances have opened up a new gold mine of audiovisual opportunity for the resourceful Bible teacher. Some of the tools we have in our hands today did not even exist in the imagination two generations ago. And other aids and equipment, which were desirable but financially impractical for the church, have been perfected and simplified, and are now within the economic reach of even the smaller church or school.

The message we teach and the persons we are teaching are the most important elements in the Bible teaching ministry. Yet the media we choose to communicate the message to those we teach can either expedite or hinder the process. In Bible teaching, the medium is *not* the message. But the medium can greatly assist or hinder the message. With our focus solidly on the message—God's written and living Word—and on the learners—young men and women God brings into our classroom—we are free to investigate and utilize any and all available means which will assist in uniting the two.

The audiovisual catalog which follows will do three things: (1) remind you of some time-honored tools which are still useful today; (2) update you on some solidly contemporary equipment and supplies; and (3) introduce you to some fairly recent newcomers in the sight, sound and feel of learning.

REMEMBER: What is true of teaching *methods* is also true of teaching *tools* — variety is the key. The same methods and tools used every week will detract from the effectiveness of the teaching experience. But using a variety of methods and tools will keep learners interested and open.

Oldies but Goodies

1. Chalkboard The classroom chalkboard remains a most economical and accessible medium for providing eye involvement for learners. It's economical because, once a chalkboard is purchased, it can render years of service without needing replacement. Purchasing a box of chalk every few months and replacing a lost eraser from time to time require minimal cash outlay. The chalkboard is accessible because wall-mounted and portable chalkboards have been standard teaching equipment for years. Most churches and schools already have a number of them.

The chalkboard can be used by teacher and learners alike for listing, outlining, illustrating and diagramming lesson material. Colored chalk can add variety and interest. Information on the chalkboard, written before the class session begins, can be hidden from view by paper taped to the board and revealed at the appropriate time.

A classroom chalkboard, frequently cleaned, well stocked with fresh chalk and creatively used, can be a primary eye-involvement tool.

2. Filmstrip projector If you are not using the filmstrip projector today because you remember these projectors to be cumbersome, noisy, difficult to load and operate, and expensive, you have a pleasant surprise coming. Filmstrip projectors are available today which are compact, quiet, easy to use and quite affordable. And there are some new materials available which make the filmstrip projector more usable than ever.

Commercially-produced filmstrips often come with soundtracks on records, but many are now available with convenient audio cassette sound tracks (cassette players are generally more portable than record players). Sound tracks from records can also be transferred to cassette tape.

Learners can make their own non-photographic filmstrips using clear filmstrip celluloid which can be purchased at many photo supply stores. Using special transparency pens, learners write or draw on the clear celluloid strip—highlighting a Bible narrative with simple pictures, listing and/or illustrating the main points in the lesson or illustrating the lyrics to a song. The celluloid can then be fed into the filmstrip projector to display the learners' work on the screen. Accompanying music or narration—live or on cassette tape—enhances the presentation.

3. Maps Unless you can afford to transport your learners to Bible lands to acquaint them with cities, countries, mountains and rivers mentioned in the Bible, you need a good supply of classroom maps. In addition to maps identifying geographic information in biblical times, each classroom needs contemporary maps showing countries which occupy biblical locations today.

Good, commercial wall maps are available in a variety of sizes, qualities and costs. Transparency maps for overhead projectors can also be purchased. A more economical approach to classroom maps—one which could include learners—is a map-making project. Learner-made maps can be as colorful and detailed as the class members like. They can also be three-dimensional—using inverted paper cups for mountains, blue cellophane strips for rivers, "Monopoly" hotels and houses for cities, etc. Learners can also make colorful and creative overhead transparency maps, using blank transparencies and transparency pens.

4. Picture file Someone once said, "A picture is worth a thousand words." The saying is especially true for the Bible teaching classroom—pictures can effectively reinforce lesson topics and principles. One way to accommodate this fact is a picture file—a collection of pictures clipped from magazines, newspapers, posters or any other source available.

A picture of skid-row derelicts to illustrate lack of direction, a war scene to portray hatred in the unregenerate heart, a child helping a friend illustration portraying the childlike love we are to have toward one another—all are pictures which can be readily found in various publications.

A teacher can train himself/herself to be alert to pictures which may be useful in the future. A picture file, organized by theme, can keep pictures ready for the right moment.

5. Record player Though many of its functions are often more easily accomplished on an audio cassette player, the record player can still assist in classroom teaching and learning. Even a modest stereo system can provide "atmosphere" for learning by playing music before, during or after the class session. Playing recorded music in order to compare lyrics with Bible principles can be done on a record player. Furthermore, recorded speeches, dramatizations and interviews can assist in driving home the point of a lesson.

Solid Contemporaries

1. Audio cassette player With the advent of efficient and economical electronics, it is possible for many churches to place an inexpensive cassette player in every classroom. A wide variety of teaching avenues is opened when a cassette player is present: a growing library of cassette tapes on Bible topics; several Scripture-on-cassette versions to use in class occasionally for Scripture reading; music for enjoyment and lyric study.

If the cassette *player* is also a *recorder*, many more options are present: in-class "radio" programs produced by learners; imaginary interviews of Bible characters and real interviews of other learners or adult church members on various topics of study. A class can use the recorder/player as a ministry tool to send a tape to a class member who has been hospitalized or has moved away, or to a missionary. Battery-operated cassette player/recorders have even greater utility for movement around the classroom, church or community.

2. Flipchart A flipchart can be as simple as a large pad of paper tacked to a bulletin board or as elaborate as a commercially-produced, wall-mounted cabinet concealing a retractable aluminum easel and paper.

The essentials are the paper and a way to display it.

A flipchart can be used, like a chalkboard, for spontaneous listing, illustrating and diagramming—with a fresh sheet of paper ready under each sheet the teacher uses. Felt markers are an inexpensive and colorful writing instrument for the flipchart—water-based markers minimize the danger of permanent staining of clothing or walls or furniture.

A carefully prepared flipchart can be an attention-keeping device during a time of teacher lecture—with each turn of the chart a new picture, diagram or illustration appears, which reinforces the teacher's message. Learners can also prepare their own flipchart presentations as part of their Scripture study. Newsprint paper is the most economical flipchart resource. It can be purchased in pads or in non-padded bulk to be stapled, taped or tacked to a useable display surface.

3. Opaque projector Though not as accessible as other media, the opaque projector offers some unique possibilities when it can be rented, borrowed or purchased. The opaque projector magnifies and projects the image of items onto a screen. It helps an entire classroom of learners see something which ordinarily would need to be passed from hand to hand to be seen. Therefore a teacher could project pages from an open book, a small map, drawing or diagram, and even a small object (signet ring, coin, etc.) for all to see. The opaque projector can be used by teachers in illustrating lecture and by learners in sharing items with the class.

Public schools which own opaque projectors can sometimes be persuaded to loan or rent their equipment for weekend use. Such an arrangement may be economically more desirable than purchasing an opaque projector.

4. Overhead projector Like the cassette player, the overhead projector is much more economically accessible to churches than when first introduced. The overhead projector uses a shadow principle to cast an enlarged image on the screen from a clear transparency marked with special transparency pens. Greater utility has been added to the overhead projector with the introduction of colored transparencies, colored pens, continuous rolls of celluloid which can be mounted on some projectors, transparency-making kits (colored transparencies, transfer letters, numbers, diagrams, symbols, etc.), overlays and professionally-produced maps, diagrams and outlines. Many photocopy machines have the capacity to produce transparencies from dark-on-light originals, making the possibilities for classroom use almost endless.

Instead of listing their discoveries on the chalkboard, learners can take blank transparencies and transparency pens and list, illustrate or diagram their assignment for projection on the classroom screen.

5. Slide projector The slide projector can be used—with professionally-produced or homemade photographic slides—to visualize for the classroom any number of items—Bible lands, current events, pictures of Bible principles being acted out, etc. Such presentations can be prepared by the teachers and/or learners outside of class for classroom presentation, or by the learners during class (arranging slides into an order corresponding to a script or outline).

Variety can be added to slide presentations by involving learners in producing non-photographic slides. Mounted blank slides, which can be written or drawn on using transparency pens, can be purchased at photo and/or school supply stores. In addition, clear adhesive material can be cut into the size of slides, peeled to expose the sticky surface and adhered to a glossy surface such as clay-base magazine paper. When the paper and clear film are firmly adhered, the slide may be placed in water to soak. After brief soaking, the paper may be rubbed off leaving the ink on the slide. The slide may then be mounted and projected, producing an interesting effect.

Learners may be given passages of Scripture or lyrics to hymns or songs to illustrate with photographic and/or non-photographic slides.

6. Listening/viewing centers Another classroom use of various cassette players and filmstrip and/or slide projectors is the listening/viewing center. Areas in the classroom can be designated as a listening center or viewing center by providing the appropriate equipment for learners to experience individually or in small groups cassette tapes, slides, filmstrips on the basis of personal interest. If the room is large enough, two or more centers may be established far enough apart from each other so as not to be disruptive. Reasonably-priced sets of headphones can be purchased and multiple jacks supplied for cassette players so that a small group of learners can listen to a cassette tape privately without disturbing the rest of the class.

Recent Newcomers

1. Marker board On the same principle as the chalkboard, the commercially-produced marker board is a smooth-surfaced, framed board which is designed to be written on with a specially prepared felt tip marker. The marker board outshines the chalkboard in that the contrast is much brighter and the colors of the markers are much more brilliant than the effect of colored chalk on the chalkboard. The marker board may be erased (providing the correct markers are used on it) with no residue of chalkdust.

2. Movies/projector As with other technological advances, the 8mm camera,

18

projector and film have come within economic reach of the Bible study classroom. If such equipment is not owned by the church or school or their constituents, it may be rented at nominal costs. Filmmaking has many of the same qualities as slidemaking, mentioned earlier, but with the added dimension of continuous action. Films may be made outside of class which will portray a Bible narrative, illustrate a principle in action or provide an open-ended drama for in-class response. As much or more actual learning may take place outside the classroom with the crew making the film as in the classroom viewing and responding to the film. A film may be a unit or quarter project, with some editing or scripting taking place in the classroom.

3. Instant print cameras Another piece of accessible photographic equipment is the instant print camera, now available in several economical models. The instant print camera can be used alone or in conjunction with a cassette player to illustrate lesson themes. Instant photos can be taken as part of an in-class or outside-of-class Bible study project as learners discuss and dramatize Bible narratives or principles. Pictures can be mounted in story strips for classroom display or in photo albums to read as books. Instant print photos are also useful to keep a record of, or display of, class members and/or class activities on a bulletin board.

4. Video cassette player Though not yet in the economic bracket of most other audiovisual tools, the video cassette player is a rising star to be considered in the Bible study classroom. Again, refinements in technology and mass production are forcing the initial costs of the video player down and many education institutions consider video taping no longer to be a luxury but a necessity. With the availability of the players comes also the availability of the cameras for classroom use, combining the values of 8mm filming with instant print photography. In-class dramatizations of Scripture, simulated TV interviews, game show format Bible quizzes and other possibilities are open when video equipment is available.

In addition, professionally-produced video cassette tapes are becoming available on countless Bible study themes. Such tapes can be used to augment in-class Bible study involvement and, in some cases, at-home learner reference.

HELP THEM SEE
WHAT YOU'RE SAYING

How to Involve Learners During Oral Presentations

Studies in learning have revealed that we retain only about 10-15 percent of what we hear. Yet much of the activity in the Bible study classroom is centered on speaking and listening—teacher to learner, learner to teacher, learner to learner. Furthermore, the venerable granddaddy of all teaching methods is the lecture— learners listen while teacher talks.

The lecture method and other methods of oral presentation in the classroom are not bad teaching methods. Often, lecture is the most efficient way of presenting a block of material in a limited amount of time, although the statistics of retention indicate that the learners come away from the lecture with significantly less than if they were more actively involved with the content.

In order to capitalize on the efficiency of the oral presentation methods without sacrificing the increased retention of more active learning methods, take advantage of a variety of oral presentation aids designed to maximize the lecture and other "up-front" presentations.

The following five categories of oral presentation aids will give the lecture-prone teacher plenty of ideas for bringing greater levels of learner involvement to oral presentation methods:

1. Audiovisuals When the teacher adds to his verbal presentation something specific for his learners to look at, the percentages of retention jump from 10-15 percent to about 50 percent. So it is most important that some kind of visual activity accompany the audio activity of listening: Listing main points on the chalkboard, flipchart or overhead transparency as they are being spoken; illustrating factual information by using large and attractive maps, graphs, charts, diagrams or pictures; visualizing lecture content with slides, films, video cassettes or objects relating to the theme. Anything that will underscore visually what the teacher is presenting orally will assist the learner in retaining a greater amount of the content.

A more thorough description of audiovisual aids available for the Bible teaching classroom will be found in the article "The Sights and Sounds of Bible Learning" on page 15 of this manual.

2. Demonstration Another way to visualize an oral presentation is to demonstrate the information or principles being verbalized. When lecturing on the contents of the Tabernacle, a teacher might prepare a model of the Tabernacle and place each piece of furniture in the model as he/she describes it. When discussing the Last Supper, the teacher may set a table in the classroom as it might have been set for the feast and indicate the location and significance of the bread and wine. The concepts of Romans 6 might be demonstrated with paper chains attached from the teacher to a person or poster representing the sin nature and another person or poster representing new life in Christ.

The demonstration adds some action to the visual element and thus increases interest and involvement.

3. Forum A forum is an open group discussion which follows an oral presentation such as a monologue, panel, Bible reading or recitation, debate or interview. Learners are encouraged to record their ideas and questions during the oral presentation and to voice these at its conclusion. A forum may be presented in a formal style with each learner giving a prepared response in turn, or in an informal style with learners dialoging with the presenters in conversational style.

Learners who are actively involved in saying and doing something in the learning process are said to retain upwards to 90 percent of the activity. Thus the activity of writing comments and questions during an oral presentation, and then talking through them during a forum period, enhances the oral presentation.

4. Question/answer As with the forum method, the question/answer method of involvement moves learners to do and say something in response to oral presentations. Several varieties of question/answer are possible: (1) Learners write questions to ask the presenter(s) at the conclusion of the presentation; (2) the presenter(s) give learners a list of questions which will be answered during the presentation, so learners listen and write answers; (3) presenter(s) may ask questions of the learners at the conclusion of the presentation to review the content; (4) presenter(s) may give learners a written quiz at the conclusion of the presentation.

5. Worksheet Another way to involve learners actively in oral presentation content is to place in their hands a worksheet and a pen or pencil with instructions as to what should be written or drawn during the presentation. The worksheet may be as simple as a blank sheet of paper for general note-taking, or as complex as a detailed outline or diagram for learners to follow and/or write on. Ample space should be provided on the worksheet for learners to write responses, answer questions, complete diagrams, etc.

Once again, the activity of writing while listening deepens the learning experience and encourages retention. The attractiveness of the worksheet can be a factor in the learners' desire to be involved. Adding artwork and using bright colored paper can invite their involvement.

It is often helpful for the worksheet to be reproduced or simulated in larger form for display in the classroom. An overhead transparency, poster or outline on the chalkboard to which the teacher refers will help the learners follow the same topics on their worksheets.

TIPS FOR GROUPING LEARNERS

Bible learning activities can be used in teaching groups as small as two and as large as can be crowded into a classroom. And within a given class period, the teacher may utilize several different groupings of learners to facilitate the lesson aims and strategies. For example, a department of 20 learners may begin a lesson in a large group completing a graffiti poster on the wall during a five-minute Approach activity. Then learners may gather for 20 minutes in three groups of six to explore and discuss Bible verses on the lesson theme. The three groups open into one large circle as each group reports their discoveries to the large group for 10 minutes. Then learners may talk in pairs for five minutes listing ways their Scripture passage might apply to teens today, and each pair returns to its group of six to share its list. Finally, individual volunteers may speak to the large group, stating their personal response to the Bible study.

Every different grouping has its value to the learning process. Large groups are most helpful during times of leader input or information sharing which is pertinent to the entire class. Small groups encourage learner interaction and involvement which is so vital to the success of an individual's learning experience. But how does a teacher know when to employ the different groupings? How can a class move from large group to pairs to small groups to large group most efficiently and with the least amount of classroom disruption?

The following tips will serve as some general guidelines for utilizing various kinds of groupings in the youth classroom:

1. Know Your Activities and Class Members

Some learning activities require a certain sized group. A group discussion works best with a group of five to eight learners and is not as productive with a group of 20 because some members will not be able to participate in a group that large. Study the requirements of each learning activity to discover the right-sized group to accomplish it. Also, be aware that some class members function best in certain sized groups. Utilize a variety of groupings which will catch the interest of the maximum number of learners.

2. Know Your Schedule and Facilities

The time schedule of a class session will suggest which groupings are appropriate for the lesson. If 10 minutes are allowed for discovering several principles from a chapter of Scripture, a teacher's illustrated summary with a large group would serve the need better than smaller groups reading, discussing, listing and reporting to the large group, which would take much longer. Classroom size, seating arrangement and facilities will also serve as clues to which groupings will be the most productive. A classroom with moveable, individual chairs will serve a number of grouping arrangements whereas fixed seating (pews, chairs bolted together, etc.) will limit grouping possibilities.

3. Avoid "Dividing" and "Separating"

When giving instructions for grouping, avoid negative and possibly threatening terms like "dividing the class" or "separating into groups." Such terms may cause learners to feel that they are being alienated from each other. Rather, suggest that learners "move" into groups of three, "gather" four chairs together, "rearrange" the circle into clusters of six or "form" pairs.

4. Give Specific Guidelines for Groupings

It is more time efficient and helpful to learners for the teacher to state specific size and location of the groups desired. Rather than saying, "Let's get into several small groups," state exactly how many groups, how many in each group and where the groups should form. "We are going to move into three groups with no more than five and no fewer than four learners in each group. One group will form by the door, one by the table and one next to the window." Often the teacher will want to preassign learners to groups based on their level of participation: "Group one will consist of Marci, Kris, Charisse and Lynette. Will you four girls move your chairs into a circle next to the table?"

5. Give Choices Where Appropriate

The teacher should decide which groupings will best suit the lesson aims, but often learners should be allowed to choose which group they will join. "We are now gathering into three work groups with no more than six in a group. You may choose which work group you would like to join—Group 1 will be working on an interview, Group 2 will do a mural and Group 3 will prepare a pantomime."

6. Give Signals for Groupings

It is often helpful to say, "When I say 'go,' move your chairs into circles of five . . . Go!" Such signals (you can create your own verbal or non-verbal 'go') will minimize movement in the classroom while valuable instructions are being given as to what learners will be doing in their new groups. Also, giving time signals during activities will help coordinate movement in class: "In two minutes we will return to our large circle . . . One minute to complete our group work . . . Now would you please open up your small circles and let's form one large circle."

7. Let the Seating Say It

Before the class session begins, arrange the chairs into the groupings which will suit the first learning activity—large circle, three rows facing front, circles of six chairs, etc. Such preparation will minimize possible confusion at the beginning of the class session as to where learners should begin. NOTE: "Circles" of chairs (5-8) often are more functional when arranged in "horseshoe" shape with the open end toward the front of the room. Such an arrangement will allow all the learners a better view of the chalkboard, screen, flipchart and leader during class work.

8. Seek Adult Leadership

Most groups of teen learners will be more productive when an adult leader is present in the group to provide guidance and assistance. The adult leader should not do all the work or give all the answers in the group, but should function as a co-learner and guide to help the group complete its task. In some situations, learners may work in pairs or trios for short periods without direct adult leadership.

9. Suggest a Starting Point

Sometimes a small study or sharing group will waste valuable time trying to decide who should speak first. The teacher can eliminate this lapse by stating in his/her instructions, " . . . and begin with the person in your group who is wearing the most blue" or "the person whose birthday is closest to today" or some other appropriate designation.

10. Give Clear Instructions

It is vital that small learning groups know exactly what is expected of them when they are formed. Unclear instructions will lead to an unproductive session. Whenever possible, write out specific, concise instructions on a card, chalkboard, flipchart or overhead transparency. Groups can then refer to the written instructions as often as necessary without needing the leader to verbalize them repeatedly.

11. Monitor Group Work

Small study or work groups, once formed and instructed, should not be left to themselves. The leader should monitor them—visit them occasionally, clarify instructions, assist with supplies, alert them as to the time remaining to work, etc. Such monitoring activity will assist groups in finishing on time.

12. Consider Permanent or Semi-Permanent Groups

While there is some value to study or work groups being formed at random each class session, permanent or semi-permanent groups meeting consistently from week to week seem to offer the best learning possibilities. In consistent groups, learners get to know one another better and are more likely to open themselves up to one another in the application of Bible principles.

13. Small Groups Must Share

One of the greater values of groups working individually is the sharing they do with the large group. A group which is given an assignment or task will be more productive if they know they will be sharing their findings or work with others in the classroom. Also, one group will benefit from hearing and seeing what another group has done. Plan to allow time for small groups to share their discoveries. NOTE: It is wise to call for groups to share in random order so that each group thinks, "We may be next, we had better pay attention."

SYMBOLIC SHAPES/DESIGNS

Purpose: To focus learners' attention on the theme of a particular Bible study session and to create an environment in which it will be easy for learners to share how they feel by using symbolic shapes or designs.

Materials
☐ A stack of newspapers and magazines
☐ Scissors
☐ Butcher paper
☐ Tape

Procedure
1. Before class, post a strip of butcher paper on the wall.
2. Invite learners to find a shape or design in the newspapers or magazines that describes a particular topic from today's Bible study session.
3. Have the learners tape their selection to the butcher paper and write their names under it.
4. Learners explain the symbolic shapes or designs they have chosen.

Variation
Send students outside to find some item symbolic of their relationship to Christ or which symbolizes something He has taught them.

The following could be used as an Approach activity in a lesson on Job:

Before class, post a strip of butcher paper on the wall. Write the following title on the paper: "My Last Week Was Like . . . " As learners arrive invite them to find a shape or design in the newspaper or magazine that describes the kind of week they have just experienced. One student might choose an arrow to show that the week went by quickly. Another student might choose a snail to show that the week went by slowly.

Getting Started
Sample teacher instructions for using Symbolic Shapes/Designs as an Approach activity:

"Look through the newspapers or magazines to find a design or advertising logo that describes your past week. Tape it to the paper on the wall. Be ready to share why you chose that particular shape or design."

Sharing Bible Learning
"I can see by the shapes and designs that you have shared that some of you had a wonderful week and others had a rather difficult week. I don't think anyone could top Job for troubles, though. Today we will take a look at the suffering Job went through and how he responded."

ART ACTIVITIES

DECISION REMINDER

Purpose: To clarify a learner's response to a biblical passage and to design a reminder for follow-through.

Materials
☐ Felt tip pens
☐ Index cards or card stock cut to size desired

Procedure
1. Lead your class through your Bible Exploration.
2. During the Conclusion, identify actions suggested by the Bible passage.
3. Distribute cards. Show an example of a completed card.
4. Learners choose an action to write on their cards.
5. Have learners make one or more reminders.
6. Instruct learners to post the cards in a place where they will see it many times during the coming week.

Variations
1. Use cartoon images to say the reminder statements.
2. Make credit card size reminder statements for learner to carry in their purses or wallets.
3. Make locker door reminder statements to use at school.

Example
If you were studying Colossians 3:3-16 you might ask your learners to make decision reminder cards with positive actions suggested on the back side.

Getting Started
Sample teacher instructions for using Decision Reminder in a Conclusion activity:

"Scripture tells us not to hear the Word only, but to take action. What is one item which we studied today that you might want to stop or start doing? I want you to make a reminder of that decision."

Sharing Bible Learning
"We've made some important decisions this morning. When you see this card, stop to consider what God has been saying to you through His Word. The more often you do that this week, the more permanent your decision will be."

26

GROUP DRAWING

Purpose: Learners work in groups to illustrate the session theme, historic events or implications of a Bible truth or event.

Materials
☐ Bible for each learner
☐ Wide point felt tip pens
☐ Butcher paper
☐ Tape

Procedure
1. Group your class into teams.
2. Tape large piece of butcher paper on the wall.
3. Learners read preselected Scripture looking for details and main idea(s).
4. Groups work together to summarize the message of the passage.
5. Each team draws a picture on butcher paper which represents the theme, events, or Bible truth discovered.
6. Groups display and explain their work for the class.

Variations
1. Students may make group time lines or histories of selected Bible characters by studying specific portions of Scripture and recording the events given there, then combining their efforts with other students.
2. Students may tape Group Drawing together to make a continuing mural.

Example
   This activity could be used in a study of Colossians 2:6,7 and Galatians 5:22,23:
   Draw the outline of a tree on the paper so the class can identify the area above and below the ground. Have both teams study the Bible passages. Ask one team to find foundational truths and the other team the results. Each team is to transfer ideas to the butcher paper as either "roots" or "fruits."

Getting Started

Sample instructions for using Group Drawing as a Bible Exploration activity:

"You have just finished studying key passages of Scripture. I want you to transfer the message you've learned to the paper on the wall so that anyone who enters our room will be able to visualize what that Scripture means."

Sharing Bible Learning

"We have discovered what the Bible teaches about fruit produced when our faith is rooted in Jesus Christ. Let's take some time to examine our own lives to see areas where we are producing fruits because of our faith in Christ."

ART ACTIVITIES

Jr. High   Sr. High

TRAFFIC SIGNS

Purpose: To help learners identify and visualize main ideas of Scripture passages.

Materials
- ☐ Bibles
- ☐ Large construction paper (11″ × 17″)
- ☐ Wide felt tip pens
- ☐ Tape

Procedure
1. Study preselected Scripture passages to identify the main ideas or messages.
2. List common traffic signs and determine their proper color.
3. As a class, decide which sign would be proper or best for each main idea.
4. Have individual learners volunteer to prepare the signs with large letters that can be read from a distance.

Variations
1. Create signs that have dual meaning such as open and closed signs. Find appropriate Scriptures to go with each message.
2. Replace signs in the chruch with signs that say the same basic thing but also have a Scripture message on them.

Example

Sign	Scripture	Message
GO	Matthew 28:19	Make disciples.
YIELD	Romans 6:19	Put God first in everything.
STOP	1 John 3:9,10	Stop sinning.
ONE WAY	John 13:34,35	Love other Christians.
CAUTION GO BACK	2 Corinthians 6:14	Don't date non-Christians.
DO NOT ENTER	Deuteronomy 18:9-14	Don't go near the occult.

Getting Started
Sample instructions for using Traffic Signs as a Bible Exploration activity:

"When I use the word 'commandments' does it bring to your mind positive or negative feelings? Explain your responses. Today we are going to list some of God's commandments and make signs to remind us of them."

29

PAPER TEARING

Purpose: To focus learners' attention and introduce the theme for a particular Bible study session.

Materials
☐ Colored construction paper
☐ Clear instructions

Procedure
1. Have table and construction paper in a permanent spot in your classroom or have chairs arranged in circles of 3-6 with paper in the center.
2. Prior to class write a significant word or phrase from the session focus on a chalkboard or overhead transparency.
3. Instruct class members to tear or fold a sheet of paper into a shape which represents something about the word.
4. Volunteers show and briefly explain their shapes to the rest of the class.

Variations
This activity can be used as part of the Conclusion section of your session. Learners would be instructed to tear a shape that represents a way they can implement the session focus or Bible truth in their lives in the coming week.

Example
If the word you choose is "inheritance" one student might fold the paper into a box-like shape and explain that it represents a treasure chest.

Getting Started
Sample instruction for using Paper Tearing in an Approach activity:
"I've written a word on the chalkboard and I would like each of you to take a sheet of construction paper and spend a couple of minutes folding or tearing it into a shape that represents to you something about this word."

Sharing Bible Learning
"We've just seen many examples of what the word 'inheritance' says to us. Today's session focuses on Israel's inheritance of land, some contrasting attitudes toward that inheritance and our spiritual inheritance as believers in Christ."

ADVERTISEMENT BROCHURE

Purpose: To put a Bible truth or phase of the Christian life into a format that allows learners to see its benefit and value to their lives.

Materials
☐ Bible for each learner
☐ Paper
☐ Felt-tip pens

Procedure
1. Learners read preselected Scripture passage, looking for main idea(s).
2. Individuals or groups, working together, discuss message of the passage.
3. Learners rough out ideas for a brochure to "sell" a predetermined quality, benefit or provision related to the Bible passage.
4. Learners construct and write brochure.
5. Learners share their Advertisement Brochure with the class.

Variations
Learners may construct more elaborate brochures by using portions of magazines, newspapers or catalogs.

Example
If your class is studying Ephesians 6:10-24 you can use an Advertisement Brochure in the following way:

After reading Ephesians 6:10-24, discussing enemies that prompt spiritual warfare today, and describing elements of spiritual armor and how armor prepares believers for spiritual warfare, the class develops an Advertisement Brochure promoting spiritual armor. Learners use supplied materials to illustrate and explain spiritual armor and ways this armor aids them in taking a stand against faces of evil today.

Getting Started
Sample teacher instructions for using Advertisement Brochure in a Bible Exploration activity:

"We have just read today's Scripture passage and worked together to list the armor that God provides His children to prepare them for spiritual warfare. Now we are going to move into small groups taking the information we have gathered and use it to make a brochure that advertises the benefits of claiming our spiritual armor. You will find paper and felt markers on the supply table."

Sharing Bible Learning
"You've all done a very creative job of preparing your brochures. Let's take a few minutes to share these projects so that we can all benefit from each other's work. Why don't we have one group member read the brochure to the class. John, would your group like to be first?"

ART ACTIVITIES

BILLBOARDS

Purpose: To help learners illustrate the session theme, events or scriptural truth.

Materials
- ☐ Bible for each learner
- ☐ Note paper
- ☐ Pens or pencils
- ☐ Large sheet of newsprint or poster board
- ☐ Felt pens
- ☐ Masking tape to post work

Procedure
1. Learners study a preselected Scripture passage listing ideas, events or details.
2. Individuals or groups write summary statements of the main idea of the passage.
3. Learners work in small groups to prepare billboards to illustrate the message of the passage.
4. Learners post and share with the class.

Variations
Create more permanent and interesting billboards by using heavy cardstock. Shapes and layers may be added for a 3-D effect.

Example

Getting Started
Sample teacher instructions for using Billboards as a Conclusion activity for a study of James:

"Turn in your Bibles to James 3:13. Let's read together through verse 17." Class reads verses together. "Now let's summarize what we've learned by listing the benefits of heavenly wisdom and the results of earthly wisdom and then creating billboards which reflect our findings."

Sharing Bible Learning
"Today we have been looking at two types of wisdom: earthly and heavenly. Your group has looked at a passage from the book of James and discovered a little about these kinds of wisdom. Let's share what we have discovered with the group. How about the earthly wisdom Billboards sharing first?"

ART ACTIVITIES

BANNERS

Purpose: To introduce and/or focus learners' thinking on the session theme or central truths by the use of banners.

Materials
- [ ] Bible for each learner
- [ ] Large sheets of paper or butcher paper
- [ ] Felt pens or paints and brushes
- [ ] Masking tape for posting

Procedure
1. Have a supply table ready with enough materials for learners to work in groups of 3 to 6.
2. Give each group a Bible passage or a specific theme for their banner. Brainstorm an idea for banner. Symbolism can be used.
3. Using butcher paper, felt pens and/or paints, the banner can be made quickly or the banner can be a session-long project or even several sessions long.
4. Learners should post banners and share their ideas and discoveries with the whole group.

Variations
1. More elaborate banners can be made using time from two sessions. Make banners with felt squares (at least 12″ × 12″) using various colors of burlap as a background and white glue to secure.
2. Oil or acrylic paints can be used.

Example

Getting Started
Sample instructions for using Banners as an Exploration activity:
"According to the following Scriptures—Psalms 19:14; 44:21; 51:10, 17; 119:11—how would you characterize David's 'heart' condition with God? We are

going to make a summary statement and design a banner which will illustrate the main idea or thought of these psalms. You may use any of the materials on the table. Be prepared to post your banner and share your findings of David's 'heart' condition in reference to his relationship with God."

Sharing Bible Learning

"A lot of good thought has gone into these banners. Let's have one person from each group summarize what the group discovered. They will have one minute. While we are sharing, be thinking about what someone might print on a banner about your 'heart' condition."

ART ACTIVITIES

MOBILE

Purpose: Learners summarize Bible learning by illustrating ideas or concepts they have learned using pictures, words or figures.

Materials
☐ Bible for each learner
☐ Construction paper and/or magazines
☐ Felt pens
☐ Hanger (for wire)
☐ Thick thread or light string
☐ Clear instructions
☐ Scissors and glue
☐ Stapler

Procedure
1. Move class into groups of 3-8 people.
2. Have one person read preselected Scripture passage and the others in the group list characteristics, ideas, attitudes or desired information.
3. Each group needs ample supplies located on table.
4. Instruct group to look through magazines or draw pictures or cut out symbols to illustrate the information they listed from Scripture research.
5. Using the wire hanger, tie two or more lengths of string with the pictures or drawings or symbols attached (use stapler) so that the whole set of pictures and string balance when hung from ceiling or light. The mobile should be able to move freely as it hangs.
6. Have each group display their mobile and share their findings with the class.

Example

Getting Started
Sample of teacher instructions for using Mobile in a Bible Exploration activity:
"Today we want to examine what kind of fruit we are growing in our lives. Let's turn to Galatians 5:16-23 and as we read I want you to list the deeds or fruit of the

flesh and the fruit or deeds of the Spirit. Now that we have our words, let's find pictures that illustrate these words. We will use the pictures to make a mobile. You will find a sample mobile hanging in front of the room. All the supplies are on the table."

Sharing Bible Learning

"Now every group should have their mobile hanging and a spokesperson for each group assigned. As we share our discoveries, I want you to think of how you demonstrate the deeds of the flesh at school or home or work. How could you demonstrate the fruit of the Spirit?"

Jr. High   Sr. High

T-SHIRT TESTIMONIES

Purpose: To reinforce the main theme of a passage of Scripture by designing a logo for a T-shirt.

Materials
- ☐ Plain T-shirt for each learner
- ☐ Butcher paper
- ☐ Crayons (special fabric crayons may be obtained at variety stores)
- ☐ Cardboard on which to pin T-shirts
- ☐ Pins
- ☐ Iron

Procedure
1. Learners read preselected Scripture and decide what they feel is the main message.
2. Learners work individually or as a group to design a logo which represents the message.
3. Each learner draws the logo on a piece of butcher paper with crayon. Students must press hard so there will be a thick layer of crayon. If words are used they must be reversed!
4. A piece of cardboard is inserted inside the T-shirt. The front of the T-shirt is pinned to the cardboard to provide a flat, smooth surface.
5. The logo is then pinned face down onto the T-shirt and a warm iron is applied to one section at a time. Be careful not to move the paper or the logo will smear!

(HINT: A cup of vinegar in the first wash water will make the design more permanent.)

Variations
The same procedure may be used to make a class banner.

Example

Getting Started

Sample teacher instructions for using T-shirt Testimonies in a Bible Exploration activity:

"We have just read Hebrews 1. What do you feel is the most important message of this chapter? How could we express this message with a simple design?"

Sharing Bible Learning

"Now let's review what our T-shirts represent by reading Hebrews 1:3. You may have a friend ask you what your T-shirt logo means. What would you tell them?"

PAPER BAG IDENTITIES

Purpose: To make it easier for learners to share their problems with each other and "carry each other's burdens."

Materials
- ☐ Bible for each learner
- ☐ Brown paper grocery bags
- ☐ Crayons or colored felt pens
- ☐ Scissors

Procedure
1. Teacher prepares sample Paper Bag Identity.
2. Learners think of images people choose to portray.
3. Learners make Paper Bag Identities of stereotypical "masks" people wear.
4. Learners share and discuss their Paper Bag Identities. Use this time to build interest in the session.

Variations
1. Roleplay may be used. Have different identities interact as they would if they were wearing that "mask."
2. If students are particularly open, have their Paper Bag Identity represent the image they sometimes portray to others. Learners can "break out of the bag" symbolically by ripping up the grocery bag.
3. Instead of using paper bags make masks of papier mâché.

Example

Getting Started
Sample teacher instructions for using Paper Bag Identities in an approach activity for a lesson on Galatians 6.

"Have you ever known someone who seemed a little phony? People sometimes wear masks with each other. Can you think of examples of images people try to portray? Think for a moment, then we will make Paper Bag Identities to represent the images people portray."

Sharing Bible Learning
"Let's share some of the identities you made. Why do you feel people try to hide their true selves? Does this make it harder or easier to help each other?

Open your Bibles to Galatians 6. Read the chapter silently, then we will see if you feel differently."

ART ACTIVITIES

BOOK COVERS

Purpose: Learners create a daily reminder of a practical application of the Scripture studied.

Materials
☐ Heavy butcher paper
☐ Pattern
☐ Felt pens
☐ Sample completed book cover

Procedure
1. Guide class in forming groups of 2 to 6 learners.
2. Complete the Bible Exploration.
3. Have the groups list various personal commitments which could be made in order to follow the Bible principle studied.
4. Learners individually choose a commitment they want to make to God.
5. Each learner decides on a phrase which will remind them of his or her commitment.
6. Cut a paper to fit a book they will take to school each day.
7. Fold paper, as shown, to the same height as the book.
8. Fold a pocket, as shown, and tuck in cover of book.
9. Stretch paper around and form another pocket to fit book cover.
10. Use cellophane tape to secure if necessary.

Variation
Students can create stickers or labels by drawing symbols or mottos on white contact paper with felt pens. The shapes are then cut out and can be applied to books which are already covered, notebooks, book bags, etc.

Examples

Scripture	Application	Book Cover
1 Thessalonians 5:17	Prayer	Talk to the Boss
Acts 1:8	Witnessing	Share the Good News
Psalm 119:9,11	Daily Bible Reading	Dig for Gold

Getting Started

Sample teacher instructions for using Book Covers in a Conclusion activity:

"We have just finished studying Acts 1:8. What have you decided about your personal witness to friends who do not know Christ? Let's make a reminder that will help you to remember at school what you have decided to do today. What phrase would remind you of the need to witness? You could use a phrase like 'Share the Good News' and illustrate it with a picture of several megaphones."

Sharing Bible Learning

"Your covers look great. They are like coded messages, reminding you of what you want to do. Others who look at them might become curious and ask you what they mean. That would be a great way to start sharing your faith with your friends."

PHOTOGRAPHIC SLIDES

Purpose: Class members graphically illustrate the truths learned from Scripture.

Materials
☐ Camera (35mm or 110)
☐ Slide film
☐ Standard slide projector
☐ Cassette recorder (optional)

Procedure
This activity requires out-of-class time.
1. Study a preselected Bible passage.
2. Select the main theme or action to be portrayed through Photographic Slides.
3. Brainstorm the kind of pictures that would best illustrate your Scripture lesson.
4. Prepare a narration (much like a filmstrip script) by writing two to four sentences per picture.
5. Arrange a time to finish the project.
6. Take pictures as planned and have them developed. Do not mix 35mm and 110 slides. Use only one format.
7. Arrange the slides in order of presentation and place in a slide tray. Preview the slides to assure that they are right-side-up.
8. Practice advancing the slides with persons who will read the script to assure a smooth presentation.

Optional: (Recorded Narration)

If you have access to a stereophonic tape recorder with separate controls for the left and right channels, you can make a professional presentation with very little extra effort. After steps 1-7 above, prepare the sound track as follows:
1. Read the narration onto the left channel only.
2. Turn the left channel off and record some appropriate music onto the right channel only.
3. Now play both channels with both music and words. Be sure to keep the music relatively low so everyone will be able to understand the words of your script.

Note: If someone in your church has a projector like the Bell and Howell Ringmaster, you can produce a cassette tape that will automatically advance the slides.

Variations
1. Depending upon the illustration being drawn from Scripture, it may be possible for slides to be taken within the class setting using props on hand, then developed and presented the following week.
2. Pictures in books and magazines can be photographed to add an unusual dimension to the slide show.

Example
Photographic slides could be used to illustrate biblical principles of the Beatitudes (Matthew 5:3-12). Slides could be taken of people in actions which

illustrate each beatitude. One person can be selected to narrate the script the group has worked on to explain each verse.

Getting Started

Sample teacher instructions for using Photographic Slides in a Bible Exploration activity:

"We are going to make a slide presentation. We have just studied the Beatitudes. Let's try to think of ways we could explain to others what we have learned. First, list the main truth of each verse." Record students' ideas. "Now let's think of the kinds of pictures we could take this week to illustrate these thoughts."

Sharing Bible Learning

"We are glad to have the College Career class visiting with our class today. We would like to share some insights we have gained into the meaning of Matthew 5:3-17 by presenting a slide show."

FILMSTRIP

Purpose: Learners prepare a filmstrip presentation to illustrate the main idea of a Scripture passage they have studied.

Materials
☐ Kodak filmstrip material
☐ Overhead transparency pens
☐ Standard filmstrip projector
☐ Cassette recorder (optional)

Procedure
1. Move class into groups of two to six.
2. Study the selected Scripture passage.
3. Prepare a narration by using phrases of two to four sentences.
4. Have the class decide on a word, symbol or simple stick figure to represent the main idea of each portion of the narration.
5. Draw the symbol on the filmstrip using the area of four sprocket holes. Leave a small margin on all four sides of this area.
6. Place the completed filmstrip in a projector. Preview all frames to make sure they are not upside-down or backwards.
7. Have a student read the narration while another advances the filmstrip.
8. Optional: Record the narration on a cassette recorder and use any sound, such as two spoons clicking together, to indicate when the frames are to be advanced.

Variations
1. This activity can be done using Kodak Ectagraphic write-on slides.
2. If you have old discarded filmstrips available you can bleach them for re-use by following the simple procedure:
   - In a cup or small bowl mix a solution of 1 part bleach to 1 part water.
   - Submerge the loosely wound filmstrip in the bleach solution.
   - After the filmstrip has been bleached, rinse it very thoroughly and air dry.

Example
In a study of Galatians 5:13-23 cartoons or stick figures could be used to illustrate serving one another in love and symbols could be used to describe the fruits of the Spirit as the narrator explains the meaning of the Scripture.

Getting Started

Sample instructions for use in a Bible Exploration activity:

"We are going to make a filmstrip presentation. We have just studied Galatians 5:13-23 and summarized the meaning of the passage. If we were to tell others what the Scripture says, what phrases would you use?" (Make a list.) "Now let's group similar ideas together into groups of two or three phrases. We want to make a very simple word or symbol to go along with each group of phrases."

Sharing Bible Learning

"What a great job our filmstrip group did. Let's watch their presentation as a review of what we learned last week in our study of Galatians."

THIS IS YOUR LIFE

Purpose: To help learners present the information, facts, character strengths of a Bible personality, or situations of a Scripture passage in dramatic form.

Materials
☐ Bible for each learner
☐ Optional: Construction paper
        Felt pens
        Costumes
        Various props (screens, chair, etc.)

Procedure
1. Have group of five to eight learners study a Scripture passage(s) and list all the information and details about the Bible character spoken of in the passage.
2. Discuss the list and the implications or impact of the Bible character.
3. Assign various students in each group roles of people who interacted with the Bible character. Have one person from each group act as the announcer/interviewer/host and one to act as the Bible character. Announcer, Bible character and other actors work out skit to present to another group.
4. Set up a stage (real or imaginary) for Announcer and Bible character to sit upon. Other actors stand behind a screen or are in some other way kept out of view.
5. Actors share important moments in their lives which involved the Bible character.
6. Announcer instructs the Bible character to try to guess who the person is who is sharing information.
7. Proceed with character testimonials until all information is shared.

Note: The learning in this activity is accomplished by the students studying the Bible characters and events in order to put on a skit. It is not meant to be a guessing game. Encourage learners to "ham it up."

Variations
1. The audience can try to guess the identity of the characters giving testimonials.
2. With various props and costumes this can be prepared over several sessions and presented as a program for another class.

Example
1. In a "This Is Your Life, Joseph" skit the characters offering testimonials might include: Jacob, Rachel, Joseph's brothers, Pharaoh, Potiphar's wife.
2. In a "This Is Your Life, David" skit the characters offering testimonials might include· Jesse, Samuel, Goliath, Saul, Abigail, Jonathan, Mephibosheth, and Solomon.

Getting Started
Sample teacher instructions for using This Is Your Life in a Bible Exploration activity studying people from the early church:
"Today we want to look at a person who is an example for our lives. Each group

will present a skit which illustrates that character's personality and strengths. Using the information found in Acts 18:22-28 and 1 Corinthians 3:1-9, prepare a 'This Is Your Life, Apollos' skit in which Paul, Priscilla, Aquilla and a member or two of the Corinthian church reflect on Apollos's characteristics, personality qualities and strengths. Prepare your skit to present to the whole group."

Sharing Bible Learning

"You get the feeling these people really know Apollos as a person. What did you learn about him? What were his strengths? In what area did he need help? In what ways can we follow Apollos's example?"

Jr. High Sr. High

DIALOGUE

Purpose: Learners present Bible facts and insights in a conversation between two or more people.

Materials
☐ Bible for each learner
☐ Optional—Props, table, screen, costumes

Procedure
1. Learners read preselected Scripture passages listing the main events, ideas, characters, etc.
2. Small groups of learners prepare a dialogue between the characters, using the events, ideas, as well as possible emotions or insights that might enliven the conversation.
3. Learners present their dialogue to the class and discuss the concepts presented.

Variations
1. Prepare an incomplete outline of the dialogue and let the learners complete it based on their Bible research.
2. List the characters to be in the dialogue on the instruction card.

Example
   The following is a partial dialogue that is based on the story of the prodigal son from Luke 15:11-32. This takes place one month after the return of the younger brother.

Elder Brother: I can't believe you ever left this good life on the farm.
Younger Brother: Me either! I guess I wanted it my way. I thought I needed independence from Dad.
Elder Brother: Tell me, what was it really like in the big city, lots of girls?
Younger Brother: It sure looks good and like lots of fun if you have the money. As long as my money lasted I had friends. But when the money ran out—so did my friends.
Elder Brother: I thought you had the good life but I guess it was a hard lesson to learn.

Getting Started
   Sample teacher instructions for using Dialogue as a Bible Exploration activity:
   "We want to find out as much as we can about the two brothers found in Luke 15:11-32. Write down everything you read about the younger and older brother and then with a partner, I want you to write a conversation between the two brothers that might have taken place after the younger brother had been back for one month. Use the insights from the passage to help you incorporate the Scripture truth into the dialogue. Be prepared to share with the class."

Sharing Bible Learning

"We would like to have each group share their conversation with the class. As each group shares, I want the remainder of the class to list biblical insights that are shared in the conversation. Listen for modern day insights, too."

DRAMA ACTIVITIES

PAPER BAG SKITS

Purpose: To help learners apply Scripture to life situations.

Materials
☐ Large brown grocery bag for every group of three to five learners
☐ Each bag contains ten totally unrelated objects to use as props and the Key Verse written on a slip of paper

Variation
1. Paper bag skits may be performed for another class.
2. Paper bags may each have a different Key Verse from previous lessons. Skits would then be a unit review.

Procedure
1. Have learners form teams of three to five.
2. Give each group instructions and a bag.
3. Learners have 10 minutes to make up a skit.
4. Teams perform skits for each other.

Example
Key Verse is Colossians 3:23 *(NIV)*. "Whatever you do, work at it with all your heart, as working for the Lord, not for men."

Bag might contain: Key Verse, car keys, onion, golf ball, tissue, doll, shoe, pencil, lipstick, wallet, screwdriver. Skit might have doctor late to visit patients (learners) because he is out playing golf (show ball), and his Cadillac (show keys) won't start. When he finally arrives, his heart is not in his work. A patient with a cold is given a tissue; one with hiccups is given an onion, etc. Skit continues until a patient says to the doctor, "Don't you know that the Bible says 'Whatever you do, work at it with all your heart, as working for the Lord, not for men'?" Doctor is penitent.

Getting Started
Sample teacher instructions for using paper bag skits as a Bible Exploration activity.

"I have put our Key Verse and ten objects in a bag. Your team must improvise a skit using all ten objects and the verse. Try to make your skit a real life situation, but feel free to exaggerate. You have 10 minutes before we'll share the skits."

Sharing Bible Learning
"You did a great job! Even though these skits might seem sort of silly, I think they can help us better understand the meaning of the verse and how it can apply to our daily lives."

DRAMA ACTIVITIES

PUPPETS

Purpose: That learners dramatize biblical events or principles through the medium of puppets.

Materials
☐ Puppets (professionally made or handmade from cloth scraps, papier-mâché or paper bags)
☐ Puppet stage (portable chalkboard, draped tables or chairs will work in place of a formal stage)
☐ Necessary props

Procedure
1. Learners read preselected passage of Scripture looking for main events or principles.
2. Learners prepare a puppet presentation (written or impromptu) which portrays a Bible event or illustrates a biblical principle.
3. Participating learners present the puppet play while other learners observe.
4. Learners discuss the events and/or principles in light of the lesson goals.
Note: Some groups may feel puppets are juvenile. One way to get around this attitude is to prepare the puppet performance for a younger class.

Variations
1. More detailed puppet plays may be prepared by learners in advance of the class session for presentation during the session.
2. Puppets may be used in conjunction with live characters in front of the puppet stage.

Examples
   The following are several ideas for using puppets in a Bible study:
1. Use puppets to reenact Bible events, such as the wedding feast at Cana in John 2:1-11 or Joseph in prison from Genesis 40 and 41.
2. Have learners employ puppets to dramatize good and bad examples of Christians responding to a biblical principle such as "do not be yoked together with unbelievers" (2 Cor. 6:14, *NIV*). Note: Often learners will find it easier to express their thoughts through the medium of a puppet than if they were speaking directly to a group.
3. Invite learners to make a paper bag puppet representative of themselves and have their puppet interact with a Christ-figure puppet in response to a specific lesson theme.

Getting Started

Sample teacher instructions for using Puppets in a Bible Exploration activity:

"What are some of the ways people respond to the principle we have been discussing today from 2 Corinthians 6:14, 'do not be yoked together with unbelievers'? For example, some people might respond by saying, 'That verse applies only to people marrying outside their faith.' What are some other ways Christians might respond? Work together in groups to discuss and list as many responses as you can think of. You have three minutes."

After three minutes regain learners' attention.

"Each group has selected a different response. Now let's dramatize the responses you have selected. On the table you will find several different puppets you may choose from. Use them to present the ideas you have discussed. As a group, put together a two-minute puppet play in which your chosen response is presented to the rest of the class. Your puppets can take the identity of a Bible study group discovering these verses for the first time, a man-on-the-street interview of several Christians responding to this principle or any other format which will help you express your response."

Sharing Bible Learning

"As I have visited your groups while you worked, I was very impressed with your creativity. You have identified several valid responses—positive and negative—to the principles concerning yoking with unbelievers. Now let's have each group present their two-minute puppet play and we will take time after each one to discuss what you have been saying to us through your presentation. Maureen, will you and your group be first?"

Maureen's group presents puppet play.

"Thank you, Maureen, Mary and Dennis. That was very well put together. Those who were watching, what response did you see portrayed in the puppet play?"

DRAMA ACTIVITIES

PANTOMIME

Purpose: That learners express their interpretation of biblical events and concepts through non-verbal action.

Materials
☐ Bible for each learner
☐ Pantomime assignments on slips of paper

Procedure
1. Learners explore Scripture to discover events or concepts to discuss.
2. Individuals or groups of learners dramatize their impression of the events or concepts through the non-verbal, exaggerated action of pantomime.
3. Learners discuss the pantomime presentations in light of the concepts presented.

Variations
1. Pantomimes may be presented for the viewers to guess the event, concept or emotion being portrayed much like that done in the game of charades.
2. Pantomime may be used to dramatize nonverbally a Scripture passage as it is being read aloud.

Examples
The following pantomime assignments were used during a lesson reviewing the life of David.
Pantomime David's attitude toward himself and God:
After he defeated Goliath
After King Saul threw a spear at him
After the death of Jonathan
After his affair with Bathsheba
On his death bed as he contemplates his life.
The following pantomime assignments were given to a group of learners acting out the Last Supper nonverbally, focusing on the feelings of the disciples during the event.
Pantomime the feelings of the following people during the Last Supper as recorded in Matthew 26:17-35:
John, the disciple who sat closest to Jesus
Judas, the betrayer
Peter, the over-confident one
Thomas, the doubter
Jesus.

Getting Started
Sample teacher instructions for using Pantomime in a Bible Exploration activity:
"Today we are concluding a study of the life of David. In looking back over his life and significant events that we looked at, we need to try to understand the feelings of the man who was referred to as 'a man after God's own heart.' We want to review five key events in David's life and see how those events affected his

attitude toward himself and toward God. May I have five volunteers who will take a pantomime assignment which will prepare us for a discussion of this man of God?

"Our five pantomime volunteers are now going to take turns portraying their interpretation of David's attitude toward himself and God after each of five events in his life. At the conclusion of the pantomime, we will take time to talk about the attitudes we have seen portrayed nonverbally through each pantomime. Bruce, would you present your interpretation of David's attitude after his successful battle with Goliath?"

Sharing Bible Learning

"Thank you, Bruce, for your portrayal of David, the victorious shepherd boy/warrior. Let's talk about what we saw. What attitudes did Bruce convey through his pantomime? What are some circumstances we face which require the same attitude of us?"

54

LISTENING TO MUSIC

Purpose: Learners evaluate the words of a song by comparing or relating them to Scripture.

Materials
- ☐ Bible for each learner
- ☐ Record of cassette player
- ☐ Records or tapes

Procedure
1. Guide class in forming groups of three to six (or use with a large group as a Conclusion activity).
2. Explain the listening assignment to the students.
3. Play a song which you have preselected for students.
4. Groups discuss the song.
5. One person from each group reports the opinions shared to the class as a whole.
6. Guide learners to compare the message of the song to Scripture.

Variations
1. Play two songs on the same subject, one from a Christian artist and the other from a non-Christian artist. Compare messages.
2. Have students bring a popular recording to class. Compare the ideas expressed in the recording to biblical truths.
3. Have students make a double list. In one column list a Bible truth. In the other, list the song phrase which related to that truth.

Example
   If you are studying 1 John 3:11-18 on the subject of loving others, play a song like "Sunday, Bloody Sunday" by U2.

Getting Started
   Sample teacher instructions for using Listening to Music in a Conclusion activity:
   "We have been studying 1 John 3:11-18 which describes our need to love and care for others. I am going to play a song for you and I want you to write down as many of the items we studied as you can find in the song.

Sharing Bible Learning
   "We have been listening to a group of musicians express their thoughts on our need to show love to others. What were your thoughts as you listened to this song? Did you feel it was expressing a biblical truth? Let's start with the group in the corner. Would one of you please respond for your group?"

HYMN/NEW WORDS

Purpose: Learners write new words to a familiar song or hymn which expresses the scriptural principles of the lesson.

Materials
☐ Bibles for each learner
☐ Writing paper
☐ Large sheet of newsprint
☐ Felt pens
☐ Hymnal or songbook

Procedure
1. Learners read a selected passage of Scripture and list the facts, characteristics, or main ideas.
2. Learners use the ideas or facts listed to write new words to a familiar tune.
3. Learners then share their song with the rest of the class.

Variations
Arranging the words of a Scripture verse to a tune can help in the memorization of the verse.

Example
1. In a study of Apollos (Acts 18:22-28 and 1 Cor. 3:1-9) new words could be written to describe his characteristics. They could be sung to the tune of "Onward Christian Soldiers."
2. Paul's missionary journeys could be detailed by writing new words to the camp tune "Rise and Shine."

Getting Started
Sample teacher instructions for using Hymn/New Words in a Bible Exploration activity:
"Today we will look at a man who provided us a great example. Read Acts 18:22-28 and 1 Corinthians 3:1-9 and list the characteristics Apollos exhibited which showed he was a man of God. Write new words to 'Onward Christian Soldiers' using your list of characteristics. Put your new words on the newsprint sheets provided. The entire class will help you sing. You have 15 minutes to complete your task."

Sharing Bible Learning
"It's obvious by your enthusiasm that you've enjoyed working on this project. Now it's time for the fun part—sharing our songs. Let's be thinking about our lives and whether someone could write the same things about us as we have written about Apollos."

CREATIVE WRITING

I AM LIKE . . .

Purpose: That learners compare their personal character traits to those of selected Bible characters.

Materials
☐ Bible for each learner
☐ Writing paper
☐ Pens or pencils

Procedure
1. Learners read a preselected passage of Scripture, looking for the main character traits of a specific Bible character.
2. Individuals complete the phrase "I am like (name of Bible character) because . . . " (or "when I . . . ").
3. Learners share their sentences in a small group and discuss the comparisons to the Bible character.

Variations
1. Learners may choose a Bible character with whom they think they share characteristics (or, with whom they desire to share characteristics).
2. Learners may complete the phrase, "I want to be like (name of Bible character) because . . . "
3. Groups list desirable characteristics of a Bible character and discuss well-known (or locally-known) contemporary figures who possess similar qualities.

Example
Genesis 24:1-67
1. Genesis 24:5—I am like Abraham's servant when I think of alternatives in case plans get changed.
2. Genesis 24:12-14—I am like Abraham's servant when I trust the Lord to guide the events of my life.
3. Genesis 24:21—I am like Abraham's servant when I patiently wait for the Lord's answer.
4. Genesis 24:26—I am like Abraham's servant when I thank God for His answers to prayer.
5. Genesis 24:33—I am like Abraham's servant when I do my chores (homework/ help with dinner, etc.) before I watch television (or go out with friends).
6. Genesis 24:56—I am like Abraham's servant when I complete what I've started.

Getting Started
Sample teacher instructions for using I Am Like . . . in a Bible Exploration activity:

"Turn in your Bibles to Genesis 24. I would like each of you to read the entire chapter, paying particular attention to the words and actions of Abraham's servant.

"After you have read the chapter, go back through the chapter and locate the passages about the servant. Look at the servant's obedience to his master, his faithfulness to God and his trust in God. Think of a time in your life when you have acted in a similar way. Write down the verse(s) you have chosen and complete this phrase in writing: 'I am like Abraham's servant when I . . . ' Then you will meet in small groups to talk about what you have written."

Sharing Bible Learning

"Form groups of three or four people. I want several volunteers in each group to share what they have written. After each person has shared, discuss what was shared by asking these questions: 'Is there a situation in my life now where I need to begin applying this lesson?' and 'When is acting in this way easier than not acting this way?'"

CREATIVE WRITING

CONTRACTS

Purpose: Learners express a commitment to a specific biblical principle studied.

Materials
☐ Bible for each learner
☐ Paper
☐ Pens or pencils
☐ Sample contract

Procedure
1. Study a preselected Scripture which suggests a response or which gives an example to be followed.
2. Lead your learners in a discussion of contracts by asking questions such as:
    Why do contracts exist?
    Who do they protect?
    How are they enforced?
3. Prepare learners for drawing up a contract in class by listing items which should be included. Show sample contract.
4. Guide a discussion of the Scripture studied. Ask learners to respond to the Scripture by writing a contract which describes a way the scriptural teaching can be applied to their lives.
5. Students write contracts.
6. Student volunteers share their contracts with the class.

Variations
1. In a study of discipleship or self-discipline students may set requirements for "graduation." They may then draw up "diplomas" upon achieving their goals.
2. Students may brainstorm ideas for tickets after studying God's promises. One such ticket might include this information:
Ticket to Heaven
Admit One Believer
Price: Already Paid
Good Through: Eternity.

Example
   The following is a driving privileges and responsibilities contract that one student drew up as a personal application for the study of Ephesians 6:1-4:

1. I will not use the car without permission.

2. I will not ask to use the car if my home responsibilities are not completed.
3. I will contribute $5.00 a week towards gas and wear and tear.
4. I will have no more than three passengers in the car.
5. I will not pay for insurance as long as I qualify for good student rates. If I do not qualify, I will pay for the entire increase which comes from adding me to my parents' insurance policy.
6. I will not pick up hitchhikers.
7. This agreement will be reviewed every six months.

Getting Started

Sample teacher instructions for using Contracts as a Conclusion activity to a study of Ephesians 6:1-4:

"We have seen in our Bible study today that God has a plan for families. We're going to apply what we've learned to our own situations by drawing up a contract. This contract can help you honor your parents by making a firm agreement with them to be responsible in a specific area. The contract will also keep you from becoming frustrated since you will know what is expected of you in advance. You may wish to write a contract agreement dealing with the use of the family car; household chores; or a time schedule for homework, responsibilities, entertainment and music or sports practice. You have 6 minutes to work on your contract."

Sharing Bible Learning

"Before we dismiss, I would like a few of you to share the contracts you have written. Who would like to begin?"

CREATIVE WRITING

WORD PICTURE CARDS

Purpose: That learners identify with a Bible character by making and sending a card which expresses an important personality trait of the character.

Materials
☐ White paper or construction paper (8½ × 11-inch) for each learner
☐ Pens, or colored felt pens

Procedure
1. Learners review the outstanding personality characteristics of the Bible character studied.
2. Learners decide on the person they would like to give or send their card to.
3. Learners make Word Picture Cards.
4. Learners share their cards in a group.
5. Learners deliver or mail their cards.

Variations
1. Students may make Word Picture Cards of the key verses.
2. Students may make Word Picture clues of different Bible characters from the quarter. Other learners try to guess the characters.
3. Learners may use index cards and make Word Picture Postcards.

Example

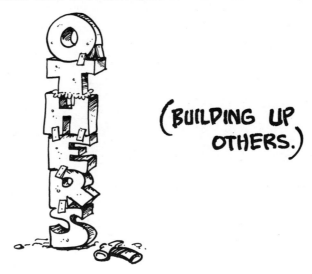

(BUILDING UP OTHERS.)

Getting Started
Sample teacher instructions for using Word Picture Cards in a Bible Exploration activity from a lesson on Barnabas:

"Turn in your Bibles to Acts 4:36. Clay, would you please read this verse aloud for us?

"It would be great to be known as an encourager. Think of some individuals you know who could be called encouragers. Can you think of people who need to be encouraged? Today we'll make a card using word pictures. Then we'll either deliver or mail the card to someone who needs to be encouraged. Take your paper and fold it in half. Here is a sample card."

Sharing Bible Learning

"Let's try to figure out what all the cards say." Learners share cards and figure out the messages. "I know from your cards that you are able to understand and do the same things as Barnabas did. Now let's consider how we can apply this knowledge to our everyday lives."

CREATIVE WRITING

HAIKU

Purpose: That learners express their understanding of a Scripture passage by writing this simple poetic form.

Materials
☐ Bible for each learner
☐ Writing paper
☐ Pens or pencils
☐ Butcher paper or chalkboard

Procedure
1. Learners read a preselected passage of Scripture to discover the main thought expressed.
2. Learners work individually or in groups of two to three to write the main thought in haiku (hī koo) form—3 lines having 5, 7 and 5 syllables respectively.
3. The poems may then be shared. Learners may compare and discuss what they felt was the main thought of the Bible passage.

Variations
1. Haiku poems may be written to capture the main message of individual chapters from the Epistles or historical events of the Bible.
2. The poems may be gathered into a collection and given as a gift to a shut-in for a class project.

Example
Haiku poem based on Psalm 8:

1	1	1	2		
Moon	and	stars	above		
1	1	1	2	1	1
Why	do	we	deserve	this	joy?
1	1	1	1	1	
You	are	a	great	God.	

(1st line, 5 syllables. 2nd line, 7 syllables   3rd line, 5 syllables)

Haiku poem written from Philippians 2:

2	1	1	1
Shining	as	bright	stars
4	1	2	
Imitating	the	Saviour.	
2	1	1	1
Rejoice	in	the	Word.

Haiku poem based on Joshua 3:

2	1	1	1	
Follow	the	Ark	now	
2	2	1	1	1
Flooding	Jordan	bows	and	parts
1	1	1	1	1
I	AM	is	with	you.

Getting Started
Sample teacher instructions for using Haiku in a Bible Exploration activity.

"In our lesson we have looked at Psalm 8. In Psalm 8, David poured out his feelings to God. What do you think he was trying to tell God? Is this something you experience today? Let's try to express that same feeling in a simple poem." Explain the haiku form to students. Write a sample on butcher paper or chalkboard. Work individually or in groups of two to three to write the haiku.

Sharing Bible Learning
"Let's compare our poems." Ask different individuals or groups to share their haikus. "I can see that different people had different ideas about what the main message of the psalm was. Why do you think this is the case? It is a wonderful fact that the Bible can speak to our individual needs. Although the message is always truth, it may speak to different people in different ways."

Jr. High | Sr. High

CHARACTER COMPARISON

Purpose: That learners compare and/or contrast personality traits, attitudes and actions of biblical characters with other biblical characters.

Materials
- ☐ Bibles for each learner
- ☐ Writing paper
- ☐ Pens or pencils

Procedure
1. Learners read preselected Scripture passages to discover information regarding the characters to be studied and compared.
2. Individuals or groups list the personality traits, attitudes and/or actions of the characters under study.
3. Learners identify similarities and/or dissimilarities between the characters.

Variations
1. Character Comparisons may be written in paragraph form with individual learners writing about one character while other learners write about other characters. Then learners read their character descriptions to each other and identify comparisons and contrasts together.
2. Character Comparisons may be written in graph form, with each chapter being described on the basis of the presence or lack of predetermined traits, attitudes or actions.
3. Biblical characters may be studied and compared to certain contemporary characters (i.e., Joseph's prison experience may be compared to the experience of contemporary Christians who have been imprisoned for their Christian stand).

Examples
Character Comparison from Luke 18:10-14 *(NIV)*:

Pharisee	Tax Collector
went up to the Temple to pray	went up to the Temple to pray
stood up	stood at a distance
prayed proudly: aloud	prayed humbly: beat his breast
thanked God for what he wasn't	confessed to God what he was
told God his good points	asked God for mercy
went home *not* justified	went home justified
exalted himself	humbled himself
humbled by God	exalted by God

Character Comparison graph from Luke 18:10-14 (NIV):

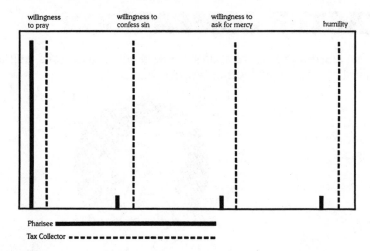

Getting Started

Sample teacher instructions for using Character Comparison in a Bible Exploration activity.

"In Luke 18:10-14 we find a parable told by Jesus describing two kinds of men and their prayers. Let's read these verses aloud together." Class reads verses.

"Now write down two headings on your worksheet: 'Pharisee' and 'Tax Collector.' I would like the two groups on the left side of the room to list all the character traits of the Pharisee—anything you see in these verses which describes his personality, attitudes or actions. Those of you on the right side of the room, you do the same for the Tax Collector. Then write your list on a large sheet of paper with a felt marker and post it on the wall on your side of the room."

Sharing Bible Learning

"Notice the two lists on the left side of the room describing the Pharisee and the two lists on the right describing the Tax Collector. Let's compare these two Bible characters by finding out how they were alike and how they were different."

CREATIVE WRITING

EDITORIAL

Purpose: That learners express the opinions of a Bible narrative or principle from the perspective of specific individuals or groups.

Materials
☐ Bibles for each learner
☐ Writing paper
☐ Pens or pencils

Procedure
1. Learners read preselected passage of Scripture.
2. Working individually or in groups, learners assume, or are assigned, the perspective of pre-selected persons or groups.
3. Learners write opinions of the Bible narrative or principle from the perspective of their assumed character(s).
4. Learners share their editorials with the class.

Variations
1. Editorials may be written on poster paper or overhead transparencies for classroom display.
2. Editorials may be presented as radio or television commentaries representing the assigned viewpoints.
3. Several Editorials may be written on one passage of Scripture from the differing perspectives of the characters involved.

Example
An Editorial written by the Sanhedrin-appointed religion editor of the *Jerusalem Journal* after the trial of Jesus recorded in Matthew 26:57-68.

April 5, 30 A.D. JERUSALEM—Once again, justice has prevailed in the efficient operation of the Sanhedrin, under the sensitive leadership of Caiaphas, the high priest. Jesus the Nazarene, who stood speechless with guilt, was appropriately convicted and sentenced to death for blasphemy last night. Witness after witness paraded to the stand and convincingly revealed Jesus for who he is—a self-deluded lunatic who thinks he is God. Never before in the history of the Sanhedrin has a case been so overwhelmingly clear and a verdict so justly decided. It was a landmark case which will forever silence the deranged Nazarene pretender and his equally-deluded followers.

Getting Started
Sample teacher instructions for using Editorial in a Bible Exploration activity:

"We know that people can have differing perspectives and opinions of the same event. Such opinions, when appearing in our newspapers, are called 'editorials.' An editorial represents the thinking of the individual writing it.

"Let's imagine that we are attending the trial of Jesus before the Sanhedrin recorded in Matthew 26:57-68, and that we have been asked to write editorials for two periodicals—the *Jerusalem Journal*, which is controlled by Caiaphas and the

Sanhedrin, and the *Carpenter's Rule*, an underground, pro-Jesus circular. Let's have one group write an editorial as it might have been written by the Sanhedrin-appointed religion editor of the *Jerusalem Journal* and our other group write from the perspective of Simon the Zealot, editor of the *Carpenter's Rule*."

Sharing Bible Learning

"Group number one, would you please read your editorial from the *Jerusalem Journal* . . . .

"What attitudes and opinions does this editorial show were held by those in the Sanhedrin? Why might they be thinking in this way?"

CREATIVE WRITING

CHARACTER IDENTIFICATION

Purpose: That learners identify similarities between themselves and Bible characters.

Materials
☐ Bibles for each learner
☐ Writing paper
☐ Pens or pencils

Procedure
1. Learners read a preselected passage of Scripture which deals with two or more Bible characters.
2. Each learner is directed to select one character from the passage who is most similar to him or her in traits or behavior.
3. Each learner writes a paragraph stating how he or she identifies with the character selected.
4. Learners read their character identifications to each other.

Variations
1. Character identifications can be written as prayers—each learner writing a prayer to God asking Him to build into his or her life the qualities observed in a character with whom he or she identifies.
2. Character identifications can be written as fan letters—each learner writing a letter to the character he or she has selected complimenting the character on traits he or she observes as similar or desirable to the learner.
3. Character identifications can be displayed by cutting out life-size silhouettes of the Bible characters involved, posting them on the walls of the classroom and having learners tape their character identifications to the silhouette of the character with whom they identified.

Example
Character identification written from Mark 10:46-52.

In the story of the healing of blind Bartimaeus, I think I am like one of the people in the crowd who tried to quiet Bartimaeus when he cried out to Jesus for mercy. Bartimaeus was desperate for Jesus to heal him, and he made a lot of noise to attract His attention. I think many in the crowd were embarrassed by Bartimaeus because they were trying to impress Jesus with their dignity and togetherness. Sometimes I am embarrassed as a Christian when other Christians are so vocal about their faith—I wonder if people will think that such Christians are weird, and then will think I'm weird because I'm a Christian too. I guess I'm too self-conscious and not God-conscious enough like Bartimaeus.

Getting Started
Sample teacher instructions for using a Character Identification in a Conclusion/ Decision activity:

"We have studied Mark 10:46-52 and discovered how different people responded to Jesus' presence among them. Bartimaeus was bold and insisted that Jesus could and would meet his need. Some in the crowd were embarrassed in Jesus' presence because they wanted to appear dignified and Bartimaeus interrupted that image. Some in the crowd apparently made little or no response—perhaps not really caring one way or another about what Jesus was doing.

"If you had been in the crowd that day, how would you have responded to Jesus' presence? Would you have been like Bartimaeus, the dignified crowd, or the uninvolved bystanders?

"Select the character or characters you identify with most in this passage and write a paragraph explaining who you are most like and why."

Sharing Bible Learning

"Let's take a few moments to allow several volunteers to read their Character Identifications to us. Let's remember that we all have room to grow and that if we admit a weakness that we see in ourselves God can help us develop strength in that area. Who would like to share first? . . .

"What is one positive quality you have observed in the characters we have studied today which you would like to develop in your life? As we close in prayer together, ask the Lord to help you develop that quality in your life."

LITANY

Purpose: That individual learners express sentences of prayer to God built around a concise statement of the lesson's theme.

Materials
☐ Writing paper
☐ Pens or pencils
☐ Chalkboard, poster paper or overhead projector and transparency

Procedure
1. Group of learners decides upon a standard prayer refrain which the group will recite in unison. The refrain is written on chalkboard, poster paper or overhead transparency for classroom display.
2. Individual learners write specific sentence prayers on the same theme as the refrain.
3. Learners recite the litany to God—one individual reading his or her sentence prayer aloud followed by the group refrain, then another individual followed by the group refrain, etc.

Variations
1. A series of different group responses may be written instead of one repeated refrain.
2. Litanies may be set to music and offered to the Lord as Antiphonal Singing.

Examples
The following is a litany—on the theme of God's faithfulness—using a standard group refrain:
Individual: Thank you, Father, for your consistency in the physical universe.
Group: Thank you for your great faithfulness, dear Lord.
Individual: I see your faithfulness in your love for me every day, in spite of my feelings or my performance as your follower.
Group: Thank you for your great faithfulness, dear Lord.
Individual: Your faithfulness is present in my family, and I see it in the way you provide for our everyday needs.
Group: Thank you for your great faithfulness, dear Lord.

The following is a litany—on the theme of God's grace—using a series of different group responses instead of one repeated refrain:
Individual: It was only by your grace, Lord, that I know your Son Jesus and am in your family today.
Group: Grace, grace, God's grace.
Individual: Thank you for the grace you showed me in sending your Son even when I was a sinner.
Group: Grace that will pardon and cleanse within.
Individual: Thank you, Lord, for by your grace my friend Barb has come to know you too.
Group: Grace, grace, God's grace.

Individual: Lord, help me to respond to your grace by walking in the good works you have created me to do.
Group: Grace that is greater than all our sin.

Getting Started

Sample teacher instructions for using a Litany in a Conclusion activity:

"We have centered our discussion today on God's faithfulness. Are you thankful that we serve a faithful Lord? Let's express our thanks to Him by choosing a simple sentence by which we as a group can tell the Lord how we appreciate His faithfulness. Here are three possible sentences we might use. Or if you have a suggestion for a group sentence, please share that with us. Let's decide now on one sentence we may use together . . .

"The sentence we have selected is a good one to tell God how much we as a group appreciate His faithfulness. But as we have studied God's Word today, you have probably discovered some elements of God's faithfulness for which you are particularly thankful. I would like each of you to write a sentence of your own expressing your thanks to God for His faithfulness to you in some area of your life. For example, you may want to thank Him for His faithfulness in helping you with school work. Let's take two minutes for you to decide on your sentence of thanks. Write it on your worksheet."

Sharing Bible Learning

"Let's now express our thanks to God for His faithfulness by reading our individual sentences of prayer aloud to Him. After each person reads their sentence prayer, let's all read together the group sentence we decided upon. We will continue alternating individual sentences with our group sentence until everyone has had an opportunity to share his or her sentence of thanks. I will begin with my sentence, then we will read our group sentence together, then Ben will read his sentence, then the group sentence, then Sarah, and so forth around the room."

DIARY/LOG/JOURNAL

Purpose: That learners express how they think a Bible character thought and felt before, during and after a biblical event.

Materials
☐ Bible for each learner
☐ Diary pages or writing paper
☐ Pens or pencils

Procedure
1. Learners read a biblical narrative describing the activity of one or more Bible characters.
2. Assign each learner or group of learners one or more characters from the narrative.
3. Learners are to imagine how their character might have thought and felt about the event in the passage and write a page in a diary—as their character might have written—with a summary of their impressions of the event.

Variations
1. The assignment may be completed as a log or journal entry—both being a daily written summary.
2. Diary, log or journal pages may be written on poster paper for classroom display.

Example
Diary entry by David after his encounter with Goliath in 1 Samuel 17:1-58:

Dear Diary,
What a super day! God used me to defeat the champion of the Philistine army—Goliath, a giant over 9 feet tall! He thought he was well protected in his armor, and he obviously didn't expect me to be much of a threat. But I got him in the forehead with the first shot from my sling—all that practice driving wolves and lions away from the sheep paid off! When he fell I ran to him, picked up his huge sword and cut off his head. What a day of triumph for Israel and our God!

The Philistines had it coming today. They should know better than to make fun of God's people. I don't know why King Saul and some of the other warriors didn't do something before I got there with lunch for my brothers. I can understand if they were scared—Goliath gave me the creeps too! But God is on our side, and I knew that if I went out in His name to do His work I could not fail. I'm glad I could be used today to defend the king and Israel, and glorify the Lord.

David Bar-Jesse

Getting Started
Sample teacher instructions for using a Diary entry in a Bible Exploration activity:
"Today's study of David and Goliath from 1 Samuel 17:1-58 will help us get a

new perspective from a familiar story to many of us. Let's recap the highlights of the story . . .

"As night fell on the Israeli camp concluding the day of Goliath's defeat, how do you think David might have felt and thought about the day's events? Imagine that four characters—David, King Saul, an Israeli soldier and a Philistine soldier—sat down at day's end to record their impressions of the day's events in their diaries. Let's work in pairs writing a 5-8 sentence diary entry as it might have been written by one of these four characters—his thoughts and feelings about the day. Refer to 1 Samuel 17 for your details. Doug and Eric, which character would you like to write about?"

Sharing Bible Learning
"Who would like to be first to read their diary page to the class?"

PRIORITIZING

Purpose: That learners express in list form a series of ideas, facts, or values in order of their importance to the learners.

Materials
☐ Writing paper or poster paper
☐ Pens, pencils, or felt markers

Procedure
1. Learners are introduced to a scriptural passage, theme, or idea which contains more than one element.
2. Individuals or groups working together arrange the elements—ideas, facts, or values—in order of their importance to the learners, and write their prioritized list on paper.
3. Learners share their lists with each other and discuss the similarities and differences of their priorities.

Variations
1. Learners may write their prioritized lists on poster paper for classroom display.
2. Learners may be asked to reduce a list of eight to ten items to three to five before prioritizing by eliminating unnecessary or less important items.
3. Learners may write each one of several items to be prioritized on a separate slip of paper. Slips of paper may be easily arranged into a prioritized list by placing them on a table or flat surface and moving them into the desired order. This may also be done with larger slips of paper on a bulletin board.
4. Learners may first brainstorm a list of facts, ideas, or values and then prioritize the list.
5. Eight to ten items to be prioritized may be written on sheets of newsprint, one item on each sheet. As learners arrive they are to mark the three items which they consider most important by a tally. After all learners have chosen, the tally marks are counted and a list is written on newsprint or chalkboard with the item receiving the most votes at the top and the others listed in descending order.

Examples
   After studying Romans 13:1-7, a group of learners brainstorm a list of authorities in the lives of teenagers (column 1). Then each small group of learners is asked to select the three most important authorities in the life of the Christian young person and list them in order of their importance in Scripture (column 2):

Column 1	Column 2
police	God
parents	parents
God	government
school officials	
self	
student leaders	
government	

After a discussion of the fruit of the Spirit, as listed in Galatians 5:22,23 (column 1), each learner was asked to list the nine elements in order of "personal growth difficulty" in their lives (example in column 2):

Column 1	Column 2
love	patience
joy	self-control
peace	gentleness
patience	love
kindness	kindness
goodness	goodness
faithfulness	faithfulness
gentleness	peace
self-control	joy

Getting Started

Sample teacher instructions for using Prioritizing in a Bible Exploration activity.

"We have read in Romans 13:1-7 that we are to submit ourselves to the authorities in our lives because God puts them there. When the Holy Spirit inspired Paul to write those words, Paul was not aware of the authorities that would be in our lives 2,000 years later. So we don't have a complete list in Scripture. But in order for us to apply this Scripture to our lives, let's brainstorm a list of all the authorities we can think of that might be included in the lives of young people today. Call them out as you think of them and I will write them on the chalkboard. Start now. Yes, police; parents, that's good. Keep thinking and calling them out . . .

"I think you have covered the subject of authorities in the lives of young people today very well. Would you agree with me that some of these are more important than others? There may be a ranking of authorities from greater to lesser. Work with your small group for five minutes selecting the top three authorities in order of their importance in the life of the teenager according to your understanding of Scripture. When we finish we will have identified the most important areas where we need to submit as instructed by Romans 13:1-8. Write your 'big three' on a sheet of newsprint for display during our discussion "

Sharing Bible Learning

"Would each group please post your list of three important authorities. Now let's have each small group explain why you prioritized your list the way you did. Shannon, why don't you tell us about your list first?

"Now as a large group let's try to decide what authority from these lists is the hardest to submit to. Derek says 'parents.' How many agree with Derek? Craig said 'God.' How many also say 'God' is the hardest authority to submit to?"

PASS THE ROCK

Purpose: To encourage participation by all learners and to stimulate their interest in the coming lesson.

Materials
☐ Clean rock 2 to 4-inches across for each six to eight learners.
☐ Paint

Procedure
1. Teacher preselects a question which will stimulate interest in the Bible lesson.
2. Before class, teacher letters question in paint on one side of the rock.
3. Group of six to eight students sit in a circle.
4. Teacher gives the rock to one student. The student may not say the question aloud, but does answer the question aloud.
5. The rest of the group tries to guess what the question is. If they cannot, the rock is passed to another person in the circle.
6. The play continues until the question is guessed, or all learners have been passed the rock and have seen the question.

Variations
1. The rock is passed to the next person in the circle instead of allowing the "rock holder" to choose. This is a good idea to use if your class has cliques.
2. The question is asked verbally. The teacher starts passing the rock. The "rock-holder" has only 30 seconds to respond. This method facilitates fast, heart-felt reactions, not well-thought-out, "right" answers.
3. This activity may be used as a game to review a lesson during the Conclusion.

Examples
Questions used before a lesson on Elijah and the widow of Zarephath (1 Kings 17:1-16).
What would you be willing to give to a newcomer to your school and why?
What would you do if someone was starving and your family had plenty of food?
What would you do if someone was starving and your family was also starving?

Getting Started
"This rock has a question printed on it. I will pass it to someone. They must silently read the question and then give as honest an answer as they can. The rest of us will try to guess what the question is. If we can't guess the question the 'rock-holder' will pass the rock to someone else and we will try again."

Sharing Bible Learning
"Most people enjoy giving gifts to friends or family when they can afford to. I think answering these questions helped us to see that giving may not be that easy if the person is not a friend or if we are giving up something we need ourselves. That is human, but is it God's standard? Let's open our Bibles to 1 Kings 17 and see if we can find the answer."

Jr. High   Sr. High

FIRST THINGS FIRST

Purpose: To provide learners with a situation in which they must respond by setting priorities based on biblical teaching.

Materials
☐ Statement of a situation
☐ Pencils or pens
☐ Paper
☐ Chalkboard and chalk or newsprint pad and felt pens

Procedure
1. Guide students in forming groups of four to six. Students sit in circles.
2. A reporter is chosen for each group. The reporter records the group's responses.
3. The situation statement is handed out, one to each group.
4. Students work as a group to set priorities.
5. Reporters report the group's responses to the class as a whole.
6. Record responses on chalkboard or newsprint pad.

Examples
Sample situations which could be used in First Things First:
1. "Remember the Sabbath day, by keeping it holy" (Exodus 20:8, *NIV*. This is a commandment of God, yet Jesus healed on the Sabbath. Are acts of mercy exempt from the commandment? How about those who must work in hospitals, pharmacies, or police and firemen? What are the Christian's work priorities in the modern world?"
2. Read Malachi 3:10. How does a Christian set priorities for his or her giving? There are many worthy para-church organizations doing the work of the Kingdom. But particular Christians have a limited amount of money for such giving. How does the Christian student set priorities for his or her giving? Should we tithe our time as well as our money? How does a Christian set priorities for his or her time between the work of the church, school, job, family, recreation, and personal growth? What does the Bible say?

Getting Started
Sample teacher instructions for using a First Things First in a Bible Exploration activity for a study of Malachi 3:10:
"We live in a complex and confusing world. There are many demands on our time, loyalty and possessions. Let's take some time today to think about establishing some guidelines for the use of these things. We will base our guidelines on God's Word."

Sharing Bible Learning
"I think this exercise has helped us to realize that it's not always easy to know the right thing to do. That is why it is important to study God's Word and spend time in prayer. Let's conclude today by thinking of specific areas in our lives where we need God's help to get things in proper order."

Jr. High Sr. High

CAN OF WORMS

Purpose: To focus attention on a particular subject and to encourage participation of learners.

Materials
☐ Coffee can (or other container to hold questions)
☐ Questions written on small pieces of paper

Procedure
1. Students form groups of six to eight. Groups sit in circles.
2. Read the Scripture to be studied.
3. Guide a discussion of the Scripture.
4. Hand a can containing questions to one learner in each group. That student draws a slip of paper from the can, reads the question aloud and responds to it. Set a time limit for how long each learner may take to respond.
5. The can is then passed to the next student who draws out a question and responds. This continues until all students have participated.

Variations
1. Bible verses may be written on the slips of paper. Learners are asked to paraphrase the Scripture in their own words.
2. Students form pairs. Disquieting situations are written on the slips of paper. Each pair of learners draws a slip and then roleplays the situation showing how a Christian should respond.

Examples
Sample questions based on a study of Matthew 6:19-24:
• A friend tells you that he can get you a job in a high-class restaurant. The hours you would be working conflict with the times of worship and fellowship at your church—but the pay is great. What should you do?
• You are trying to decide what to do with your life. Most of your friends are choosing professions based on how much pay they will receive. What should be the basis of your decision?
• You have just inherited over one million dollars from your rich aunt. What will you do with the money?
• A kid in school never has a lunch. You have heard that it is because his family is poor. What could you do?
• You have saved up enough money to buy a new car. Some of your friends want you to buy a flashy turbo-charged sports car, other friends are encouraging you to get an inexpensive model that will provide reliable transportation and use the money you save for a worthwhile cause. What would you decide?

Getting Started
Sample teacher instructions for using Can of Worms in a Bible Exploration activity:
"We've been discussing what Jesus had to say about the foolishness of putting

our hope in worldly things rather than building up treasures in heaven. Now we are going to explore how this applies to true-to-life situations. I am going to give each of your groups a coffee can containing questions you might encounter. Take turns drawing a slip of paper out of the can and answering the question on it. Remember the principles we have talked about and let them influence your answers."

Sharing Bible Learning

"I noticed some of you struggling with your responses, and that's okay. I struggle with these questions also. But I am interested to hear how some of you responded. Who would like to share an answer?

"I am impressed with your answers. Now let's take a few moments to think of ways we can use what we've learned in our everyday lives."

Jr. High   Sr. High

RESPONSE TEAMS

Purpose: To encourage learners to develop listening skills and to clarify terms and concepts used in church situations.

Materials
☐ Paper
☐ Pens or pencils

Procedure
1. Arrange to have a speaker come to class to give a mini-sermon on a passage of Scripture or scriptural theme which the class is studying. The speaker could be an associate pastor, Sunday School teacher, elder or any other person well versed in the Bible and comfortable fielding questions.
2. Group the class into two divisions. One group will listen for **terms** they do not understand. The other group will listen for **concepts** they do not understand.
3. Guest speaker gives mini-sermon on preselected topic. As he or she speaks learners listen for **terms** or **concepts** that need clarification. They note their questions on paper.
4. Time is set aside for students to ask their questions when the speaker has finished speaking.

Variations
Students listen to a short video-recorded sermon and write down questions as they listen. Following the sermon they use Bibles, Bible dictionaries and concordances to research the answers. Learners share what they have learned.

Getting Started
Sample teacher instructions for using Response Teams in a Bible Exploration activity:

"We have a special guest with us today. Pastor Johnson has agreed to give us a mini-sermon on spiritual gifts. Although we have been studying this in class, he may use some terms or speak of some things you do not understand. Please note your questions on the paper provided. Pastor Johnson has agreed to answer all of your questions when he has finished his talk. Remember your listening assignments."

Sharing Bible Learning
"I think this has been a good time of learning for all of us. I realize now that I sometimes use terms you do not understand and I think this has given you an opportunity to have some of these words and concepts clarified."

CASE STUDY

Purpose: To give learners an opportunity to apply scriptural truths to real life situations.

Materials
☐ Bible for each learner
☐ Case study for each group of three to six learners
☐ Paper
☐ Pens or pencils

Procedure
1. Before class prepare case studies. The studies are to be short stories which pose a dilemma for students to solve. A good source is the daily newspaper. Select Scriptures which will help students solve the case study. Note Scripture references on slips of paper.
2. Guide class in forming groups of three to six.
3. Give each group a case study and Scripture reference(s).
4. Groups read the Scripture and the case study, then brainstorm a solution. One person in each group takes notes.
5. Groups share their solutions with the class as a whole.
6. Lead the class in a discussion which evaluates each solution to assure that it is compatible with Scripture.

Variations
Give each group a Case Study but withhold Scripture references. Hand out appropriate references after groups have reached a solution to the problem posed in the Case Study. Groups read the Bible passage and compare the solutions they reached to scriptural truth.

Example
Sample Case Study for a study of "showing God's love":

The administrators at Central High are having a problem. There are so many cliques at school that new kids have a hard time adjusting.

A new student, Jane, has come to Central from another area of the country. She dresses differently and has an accent. Your friends don't like her because she is different. You are standing with your group of friends as they begin to make fun of Jane. Tears come to Jane's eyes. What should you do? The Scripture references are James 2:1-9 and Ephesians 4:2-6.

Getting Started
Sample teacher instructions for using Case Study as a Bible Exploration activity:

"During this unit we have been talking about different aspects of showing God's love to others. As we have discussed the principles, we have been learning how to practice these principles in our daily life. Let's investigate some specific cases that would allow us to show God's love to another person. I have given your groups Case Studies and Scripture references to read. Work as a group to solve the problem

82

in the Case Study. One person in each group should take notes."

Sharing Bible Learning

"Good work! Many of you contributed helpful suggestions for solving sticky problems. Now let's compare your solutions with the Bible references you were given. We need to be sure that the solutions are consistent with God's Word or they will not work in the long run."

Jr. High ▼ Sr. High

TALKBACK

Purpose: To encourage more careful observation of films, demonstrations, lectures, or other media to which learners may be exposed.

Materials
☐ Film or other presentation
☐ Handout sheet
☐ Pens or pencils

Procedure
1. Before class prepare a handout sheet which lists a series of questions appropriate for the topic presented. Include scriptural themes.
2. Distribute Talkback handout sheets to class.
3. Show film or other presentation.
4. Students note their answers on the sheet as the film (presentation) proceeds.
5. Discuss responses.

Variations
1. The questions may be distributed after the showing. They are answered from memory.
2. The questions may be responded to on the basis of individual opinion, neighbor-nudging, buzz groups, small or large groups, or any combination of these.

Examples
Sample groupings and questions for a Talkback based on a film on missions:

Grouping	Questions
Individuals	Name one new thing you learned. What impressed you the most? What was the main message? How does this film relate to you?
Neighbor-Nudge	How did you feel about the missionaries' life-style? Work? What impressed you the most?
Buzz Groups	What was the main message of this film? What does this film have to say about the way we should share our faith? What should the role of the missionary be in the world today? What do missionaries expect of students like us?
Small/Large Groups	What is the spiritual significance of this film? What are the implications of its message to us as Christians? How would you describe the role of the missionary in the twentieth century?

Getting Started

Sample teacher instructions for using Talkback in a Bible Exploration activity.

"We have been discussing sharing our faith with others. Many of us rely on others to do this work. We send our money to distant places. But did you know that many missionaries work right here? Let's take a few minutes to watch a short film on home missions. I have handed out sheets with a few questions listed on them. After the film we will discuss your responses to these questions, so watch and listen carefully."

Sharing Bible Learning

"I am impressed with the responses you have shared—all of them were very thoughtful. You listened well. Now let's get into the Scripture together so we can find the answers God has provided for these questions."

FILM REVIEW

Purpose: That learners investigate specific films relevant to the lesson or unit theme prior to the class or during the unit.

Materials
☐ Review sheets
☐ Pens or pencils

Procedure
1. Teacher determines specific films which will complement lesson or unit theme and prepares copies of the Film Review sheet for learners who will be involved.
2. Learners view movies and complete Movie Review sheets.
3. Learners share their reviews with the rest of the class.

Variations
1. Learners may review books or records.
2. Video equipment may be brought into the classroom. The whole class may view and respond to a short feature film.

Example
One class of learners was involved in a study of Christian life-styles. During the unit of study several movies were recommended to the learners. Some of these movies were "Chariots of Fire," "Joni," and "Good Clean Fun" (a sports film by Olson/Bundschuh Filmworks). Volunteers viewed the movies, answered the questions on the Film Review sheets, and presented their reviews to the class as reports.

Sample Film Review sheet:

Film Review Sheet

_____

Name of Reviewer

_____

Name of film (book, recording, etc.)

Main theme of the film (book, recording, etc.): _____

_____

_____

Reaction to the film (book, recording, etc.): _____

_____

_____

I would ☐   would not ☐   recommend this film (book, recording, etc.).

Why? _____

_____

Getting Started

Sample teacher instructions for using Film Review in a Conclusion activity:

"As we continue our study of Christian life-styles we will be looking at how we can express our faith to others through the way we live. I've selected several films which might give us some insight into this topic. I'd like several people to volunteer to see the films, fill out a review sheet and report their findings to the class next week. Who would like to see the film 'Good Clean Fun'?"

Sharing Bible Learning

"I'd like to thank you for sharing your Film Review with us. The film 'Good Clean Fun' seems to emphasize the variety of fun and wholesome experiences God has provided for us to enjoy. Knowing this, what should our response be?"

RESEARCH ACTIVITIES

Jr. High Sr. High

QUESTION BOX

Purpose: That learners develop skill in researching and answering difficult questions on the Bible.

Materials
☐ Bibles for each learner
☐ Research materials (concordance, Bible dictionary or other appropriate reference materials)
☐ Index cards
☐ Container for cards

Procedure
1. Select and invite to class a person who feels comfortable answering difficult questions on the Bible.
2. Prior to the day your guest will be present, your class needs to: develop a box of questions using one of these methods:
   • Ask your learners to interview a variety of students at school (both Christian and non-Christian) and ask, "What is the most difficult question about the Bible you can think of?"
   • Learners use the same procedure as above but with adults at your church.
   • Develop your own questions from ideas learners share in class.
3. Questions are written on index cards and put into the Question Box.
4. Assign several questions to each learner to research before guest arrives.
On the day your guest is present:
5. Learners ask questions on a rotating basis.
6. Guest answers questions.
7. Students share what they have learned.

Examples
A Question Box from one class contained these questions:
   • How could Jesus be in the grave three days and three nights if He was crucified on Friday?
   • Where did Cain get his wife?
   • Are people who have never heard of Jesus lost?
   • Why do people have to suffer?
   • Why are there some inconsistencies in numbers in the Bible?
   • Why did God prefer Abel's sacrifice to Cain's?

Variations
Each class session a question to be researched in the coming week is drawn from the box. Students work individually during the week to find the answer to the question. Students share what they have learned in the next class session.

Getting Started
Sample teacher instructions for using Queston Box in a Bible Explorationactivity:
"We have been studying the authority of Scripture and how we need to look to

God's Word for answers to problems which may occur in our lives. We are going to dig into some difficult questions in the coming weeks. These are questions which you may have yourself, or that you may one day be asked by a non-Christian. The answers are all in the Bible, but we need to learn where and how to find them. We will be having a special guest in our class in a few weeks. This person has spent a great deal of time studying the Scripture. Let's compile a box of difficult questions so that our guest can help us find the answers."

Sharing Bible Learning

"You have heard a wealth of information in answer to some pretty difficult questions from the Bible. I hope you have learned some skills that you will find useful from your own personal research. Can anyone summarize the main goal of our research project?"

ORAL PRESENTATION

SCREENED SPEECH

Purpose: To draw upon the resources of an expert in a given field and to guide his comments in the direction of the class' needs.

Materials
☐ A series of questions developed by the class
☐ An expert who will agree to answer the questions

Procedure
1. Learners prepare a series of questions on a given subject.
2. Give these questions to the expert in advance.
3. Expert presents discussion/lecture based on the questions.

Variations
1. A discussion may follow the expert's presentation. This gives learners an opportunity to ask questions which the presentation may have raised.
2. The Response Team approach might be used in connection with the presentation.
3. An evaluation sheet might be used to determine how well the questions were answered.

Example
1. A series of questions on the Holy Spirit might be prepared, asking how He works, what His responsibilities are, if we can see evidence of His presence in the Old Testament, etc.
2. A series of questions on the family might be developed using Colossians 3:19-21 as the base.
3. Enlist a speaker who is an expert on the subject of being considerate. The expert should be able to relate being considerate to the students' Christian walk.

Getting Started
Sample teacher instructions for using Screened Speech in a Bible Exploration activity:

"Today we have a special guest speaker. She has prepared a short talk on the subject of being considerate from the questions we wrote last week. Listen for the answers and for any new questions you might have. We will have a time for discussion following the speech."

Sharing Bible Learning
"Let's summarize what we have learned about being considerate and how this ties in with the Scripture we are studying. I'll list biblical principles on the board. I'd like a volunteer to suggest a rule for being considerate which ties in with it."

DEBATE

Purpose: To stimulate interest by presenting opposing viewpoints on a subject. To encourage learners to use the Bible to support their opinions.

Materials
☐ Bibles for each learner
☐ Concordances, Bible dictionaries or other Bible reference materials
☐ Note paper
☐ Pens or pencils
☐ Stopwatch or other watch which displays seconds

Procedure
1. A subject which is relevant to your lesson or unit is chosen. Controversial subjects or those in which the world holds one opinion and Christian believers hold another work well. One team may support the Christian point of view while the other team plays the role of devil's advocate.
2. Three or four debaters are chosen for each side. One learner is designated to be the moderator. Another learner is chosen to be the timekeeper.
3. Debaters are given time to prepare their presentations. They should take notes as they discuss their position. Learners should use the Bible as a reference, finding verses which support their viewpoint.
4. Moderator introduces teams and gives 1-minute background to the topic.
5. Teams present their viewpoints in this manner:
   - One team is chosen to go first. This team's first speaker is given two minutes to present a point. The timekeeper signals when time is up.
   - The opposing team's first speaker is then given two minutes to present the opposing point of view.
   - The debate continues alternating time between the two teams until all team members have had an opportunity to speak for two minutes.
   - Each team member is given one minute for rebuttal. Rebuttal time alternates between the two teams (usually in reverse order from that of speaking).
   - An open discussion may follow the debate.
   - Teacher summarizes the information the debate teams have given.

Variations

1. Debate teams may be chosen during class time to present arguments the following week. Learners research information during the week instead of during class time.
2. Debates between two classes may be held.
3. Evaluation sheets may be given to listening students. Following the debate students vote for the team which has presented the best argument.

Example

Some statements you may use as the basis for a debate are:

- A child must *always* obey his or her parents.
- The problems which plague us are some of God's best opportunities to enter our lives in a dramatic way.
- A Christian should not associate with non-Christians.
- A Christian should never be anxious.
- A Christian should never work on the Sabbath.
- A Christian should not try to become rich.
- Women should not hold leadership roles in the church.

Getting Started

Sample teacher instructions for using a debate in a Bible Exploration activity:

"During this unit we have been talking about principles of sharing our faith in Christ as presented in Scripture. It would seem to be obvious that we could only share our faith with others if we associate with non-Christians. Some people, however, believe that Christians should not keep company with non-Christians. There are logical reasons for both of these opinions. Let's explore them further by having a debate. We will need three or four people to represent each viewpoint. The debaters will need to find biblical support for their points of view. I've brought in some concordances and Bible dictionaries to help. Who would like to support the proposal that Christians should not associate with non-Christians?"

Sharing Bible Learning

"Good debate! Thank you for your helpful insight into a controversial matter. I think this debate has helped us see why the Bible has given us careful instructions for our conduct and for witnessing. We must be deeply rooted in the Word before we are able to share with others. I think we can see more clearly some of the pitfalls of associating with people who have a different perspective on life than we do as Christians. But, clearly we are commanded to 'go into all the world and preach the gospel.' Let's summarize what we have learned by making a list of things to remember when we are with non-Christians."

Jr. High Sr. High

BIBLE MATCH GAME

Purpose: To encourage learners to remember the ideas, concepts, or principles of the lesson studied.

Materials
☐ Large poster board with movable flaps (see illustration)
☐ Felt pens
☐ Paper
☐ Tape

Procedure
1. Before class, prepare Bible Match Game board (see illustration) using questions from the lesson or unit being studied. Number the flaps.
2. Guide learners in forming teams of two to four.
3. The teacher (or learner emcee) reads a question. Learners from the team selected to go first try to guess the location of the answer by calling out the number of one of the flaps on the game board. If the team succeeds in uncovering the correct answer, they score one point and get another turn. If the first team does not choose the correct flap the other team gets a turn. The fun comes in trying to remember which flaps cover which answers.
4. The team with the most points wins.

Variations
1. Learners may create a Bible Match Game board for a competing team or another class.
2. Questions and answers may be hidden under flaps of a large game board. Learners try to match questions and answers.

Example
The illustration below shows a Bible Match Game board that could be used for a study of the characteristics of Christ:

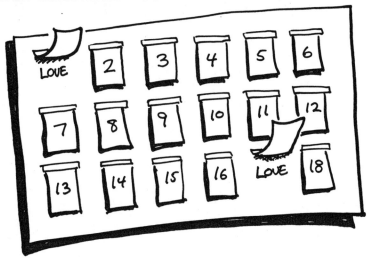

Getting Started

Sample teacher instructions for using Bible Match Game in a Bible Exploration activity:

"We have just finished a study of the characteristics of Christ. Let's see if you can match the characteristic given with the event in Christ's life which best illustrates it.

Sharing Bible Learning

"Now that we have reviewed some of the great characteristics of Christ in a fun way, let's share which of His characteristics impress us the most. Be thinking about which characteristic needs to be developed in your life."

PUZZLES AND GAMES

MYSTERY DRAWINGS

Purpose: To stimulate interest in a topic.

Materials
☐ Bibles
☐ Bible dictionary
☐ Large sheets of newsprint
☐ Felt pens

Procedure
1. Before class:
   - Select an item from your Bible lesson which can be simply illustrated.
   - Use a Bible dictionary or similar reference to find pictures of the object.
   - Plan verbal instructions for the illustrator.
2. During class time:
   - Tape a sheet of newsprint to the wall.
   - Ask for a volunteer (or you select a learner) to make a mystery drawing.
   - Read step-by-step instructions aloud. Pause occasionally to allow time for the class to guess what the object being drawn is.
   - Continue verbal instructions and drawing until someone solves the mystery.

Example
These sample instructions for a Mystery Drawing of a candlestick were used in a study of the building of the Tabernacle (Ex. 35–39):
   - Draw two parallel vertical lines one inch apart and six inches long.
   - Draw a quarter circle from the top of each line. Have the curved lines move away from each other ending six inches above the parallel lines and twelve inches apart.
   - Draw six U-shaped lines inside the curve. Position the U's so that all vertical lines are the same height.
   - Connect every two vertical lines with a small circle at the top.

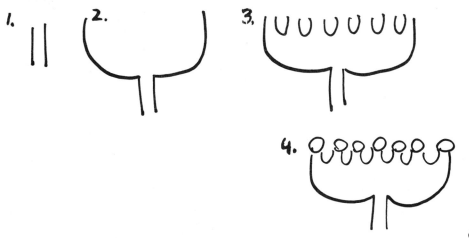

Variation

Before class cut out shapes which when assembled properly will represent an object from the Bible lesson being studied. At the start of class several learners are given pieces of the "puzzle." They must pin the pieces together on a corkboard or bulletin board to discover the "mystery object."

Getting Started

Sample teacher instructions for using Mystery Drawing as an Approach activity:

"I need a volunteer who wants to have some fun. Good, come up here Marcia. I am going to give you some instructions and I want you to follow them as closely as you can. You will be drawing on this newsprint sheet. I want the rest of you to try to guess what our 'artist' is drawing."

Sharing Bible Learning

"Who guessed candlestick? You are right. The Mystery Drawing is that of a candlestick. For us this is just a fun way to introduce a lesson. But imagine how Moses felt. He was given a very specific set of instructions from God. The instructions detailed how God wanted the Tabernacle to be built. Let's look in our Bibles to see exactly what these instructions were. Open your Bibles to Exodus 35."

MISSING WORDS

Purpose: That learners discover key words or themes in Scripture which relate to the lesson goals.

Materials
☐ A copy of the missing word puzzle for each learner (photocopied or mimeographed)
☐ Pens or pencils
☐ Bible for each learner

Procedure
1. Learners are given copies of the missing word puzzle and directed to use their Bibles to locate the verses given.
2. Individuals or groups working together solve the puzzle by finding the missing words.
3. Learners use their completed puzzles as a basis for discussion of the Bible passage.

Variations
1. One large Missing Word puzzle may be reproduced on a sheet of poster paper or on the chalkboard so the entire class may work on solving it together.
2. Missing Word puzzles may be used as review quizzes with learners identifying the missing words from memory without the aid of their Bibles.

Example
The following Missing Word puzzle helped learners identify the key words in four sections of Colossians 1.

Select the answer which correctly fills in the blank(s) in each verse. Quotations are from the *New American Standard Bible*.

1. "For He delivered us from the domain of _____, and transferred us to the kingdom of His beloved _____, in whom we have redemption, the forgiveness of sins" (Col. 1:13,14).
    a. darkness/Son   *b. sin/Saviour*   *c. sinners/followers*

2. "He (Christ) is also the head of the body, the _____; and He is the beginning, the first-born from the _____; so that He Himself might come to have _____ _____ in everything" (Col. 1:18).
    a. church/grave/God's will   *b. Lord/beginning/all glory*   *c. church/dead/first place*

3. "For it was the Father's good pleasure for all the _____ to dwell in Him, and through Him to _____ all things to Himself, having made peace through the blood of His cross" (Col. 1:19,20).
    a. fulness/reconcile   *b. world/gather*   *c. glory/present*

4. "To whom God willed to make known what is the riches of the glory of this
_____ among the _____, which is Christ in you, the
_____ of glory" (Col. 1:27).

    a. mystery/Gentiles/hope   *b. salvation/church/promise*   *c. inheritance/
believers/joy*

Getting Started

Sample teacher instructions for using Missing Words in a Bible Exploration activity:

"Today we are looking at Colossians 1. In order to learn some of the key thoughts in the chapter and prepare us for a discussion of some of these thoughts, I would like you to search through Colossians 1 and look for the correct answers for the Missing Word puzzle on your worksheet. Work individually for three minutes. Even though your version of the Bible may not be the same as the Missing Word puzzle, I think a careful look at your version will be enough to help you complete the task." Regain students' attention after three minutes. "Time is up for individual work. Now I would like everyone to select a partner and compare notes. Check your answers with your partner's answers. You have two minutes to visit with your partners."

Sharing Bible Learning

"What did you find to be the correct answer for question 1 from Colossians 1:13,14? 'A' is correct. The writer of Colossians makes clear early in his letter just what God has done for us—taken us from darkness and brought us into a relationship with His Son. What is meant by the phrase 'domain of darkness'?"

HIDDEN WORDS

Purpose: That learners learn or review key words and/or phrases for a lesson by solving a hidden word puzzle.

Materials
☐ A copy of the hidden word puzzle for each learner (photocopied or mimeographed)
☐ Pens or pencils

Procedure
1. Teacher prepares a hidden word puzzle in advance which will involve the learners in key words or phrases for the lesson.
2. Individuals or groups of learners working together solve the hidden word puzzle.
3. Learners discuss the key words and phrases from the puzzle as they relate to the session theme.

Variations
1. One large hidden word puzzle may be produced on a large sheet of poster paper or on the chalkboard so the entire class can work at solving it together.
2. Hidden Word puzzles can conceal an entire verse or key statement from the lesson.

Example

gospel	justified	flesh	Christ	love
Gentile	law	crucified	tutor	fruit of
circumcision	faith	Spirit	adoption	the Spirit
Jew	promise	Abraham	freedom	bear one
				another's
				burdens

```
B  J  R  O  X  N  W  F  T  Y  E  C  B  M  T  E  E  T  Y  N  A  I  P  B  X
U  U  O  T  Z  C  R  O  S  S  T  M  P  Q  U  T  U  T  O  R  S  T  T  V  Y
W  S  P  I  R  I  T  N  Q  T  T  U  X  F  M  I  L  I  T  F  G  H  E  E  E
Y  T  S  N  T  B  E  A  R  O  N  E  A  L  B  Q  T  X  J  Y  T  W  M  N  Z
O  I  I  O  Z  F  B  I  U  T  R  A  L  C  N  Q  P  R  O  M  I  S  E  U  L
P  F  U  L  D  D  G  H  L  S  B  V  D  V  O  M  R  Q  A  O  O  I  N  W  T
B  I  C  D  E  A  T  T  I  L  R  M  O  D  F  T  K  F  D  G  V  W  O  I  Z
G  E  N  T  I  L  E  T  G  H  A  T  A  L  S  C  H  L  I  T  Q  B  I  M  N
X  D  E  D  O  N  N  F  T  H  Z  T  Q  Y  W  C  E  K  K  N  P  X  Y  Z
S  I  S  L  M  T  V  M  R  O  A  T  W  U  U  Z  K  S  R  S  S  M  S  E  T
K  I  B  Z  N  C  I  R  C  U  M  C  I  S  I  O  N  H  V  S  Q  L  O  V  E
F  R  E  G  C  R  U  C  I  F  I  E  D  N  M  G  B  L  T  B  T  G  L  A  W
K  L  U  F  M  U  K  Y  T  O  I  T  G  R  U  F  N  U  N  U  X  E  M  C  T
Z  E  R  N  R  S  T  R  M  S  H  R  O  F  T  H  E  S  S  R  T  C  G  R  S
A  L  O  M  M  E  L  Y  T  H  M  E  S  H  N  K  C  P  D  D  T  H  M  K  T
C  S  O  M  T  C  E  F  O  T  P  K  P  D  F  K  B  I  H  E  J  R  S  M  N
H  H  W  O  K  W  B  D  R  M  K  O  E  N  M  D  T  R  J  N  X  I  T  W  T
I  T  J  E  W  N  Q  M  O  K  E  W  L  U  W  E  X  I  H  S  L  S  E  J  E
Z  G  E  L  R  N  Z  S  O  M  T  W  D  I  X  M  I  T  F  O  P  T  F  Q  Z
M  N  X  K  S  T  A  T  N  B  Y  F  W  E  Y  M  D  A  O  J  Q  J  N  O  N
```

The hidden word puzzle contains key words from a study of the book of Galatians. This puzzle was used as a final session review of a 12-week study. Note the word list at the top of the puzzle.

Getting Started

Sample teacher instructions for using a Hidden Word puzzle in a Bible Exploration activity:

"Our 12-week study of the letter to the Galatians has slipped by quickly. I have enjoyed very much learning with you the things that God has taught us about our life of liberty in Him. In order to draw all the loose ends of our study together and summarize the highlights of the book we are going to review Galatians today. One way to hit the highlights of the book is to look at the major topics. To help us do that in an interesting way, several of the key words and phrases of the Galatians study are hidden in the puzzle you see on your worksheet. Work together in groups of three to find as many of the key words as you can in four minutes. Then we will talk about some of the themes of Galatians. Have you found your partners? Go!"

Sharing Bible Learning

"It looks like John, Pat and Greg have located most of the key words. Now let's talk about some of the themes of this book. One of the words from the list is 'gospel.' You'll remember that God revealed to Paul that he had been chosen for the specific task of sharing the gospel with the Gentiles . . . . "

SELF-EVALUATION

Purpose: To help learners personalize Scripture by making positive decisions for improving their walk with the Lord.

Materials
☐ Bible for each learner
☐ Evaluation sheets (see illustration)

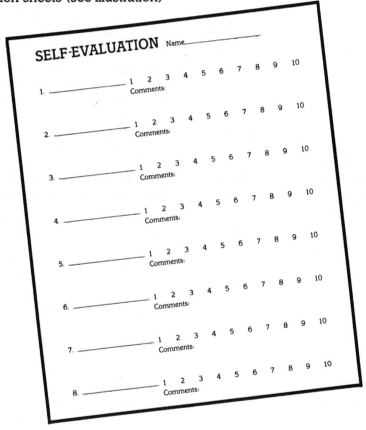

Procedure
1. Study your Scripture passage and identify parts which suggest action. Be sure that learners understand the terms used.
2. Give each learner two evaluation sheets.
3. Each learner chooses actions from the Scripture studied and prints them on his or her evaluation sheet. These should be actions which need to be incorporated into learners' life-styles.
4. Learners evaluate how closely they are living to the biblical stand given.
5. Students keep one copy of the evaluation sheet. Invite them to give the other copy to you.
6. Check with learners in several weeks to see how well they have been able to improve in the actions they chose.

Example

You may choose to study Ephesians 4:17-32 and list all "put off" and "put on" statements on the evaluation sheet.

Variations

1. Ask students to grade themselves at the beginning of the lesson. At the conclusion of the lesson ask students to evaluate themselves again. Compare th results of the two sheets.
2. Have students address evaluations to themselves. They are mailed home to serve as a reminder later in the week.

Getting Started

Sample teacher instructions for using Self-Evaluation as a Conclusion activity:

"We have been studying Ephesians 4:17-32. Perhaps God has caused several things in the passage to 'jump out' at you. I am going to ask you to choose eight actions given in this Scripture passage. Pick out four that you should put on and four that you should put off. List those on your evaluation sheet. I will not ask you to share these with each other. This is a private list. Then I want you to evaluate how you feel you have been doing in each area."

Sharing Bible Learning

"I have given you two copies of the Self-Evaluation worksheet. If you want me to help keep you on track, give me one copy. I promise you that I will not share this information with anyone."

PICTURE CAPTIONS

Purpose: Learners reinforce their knowledge of Scripture by matching Scripture passages with pictures.

Materials
- ☐ Bible for each learner
- ☐ Baby pictures of learners
- ☐ Heavy paper for backing
- ☐ Rubber cement
- ☐ Small strips of paper for captions
- ☐ Pens or fine tip felt pens

Procedure
1. One week before this activity ask learners to bring baby pictures of themselves to the next class session.
2. Class makes list of captions by paraphrasing the Scripture studied.
3. Students choose a caption which seems to go with their pictures. The caption is written on a small strip of paper.
4. Pictures and captions are mounted on heavy paper.
5. Students share their Picture Captions with the rest of the class.
6. Picture Captions are posted on the wall.

Example
Sample phrases could be:

"One step at a time, I'm heading for the goal!" Philippians 3:13-14

"I know I'm a Christian because I love other Christians." 1 John 3:14

"I'm ready to go to heaven." John 14:3

Variation

Use pictures of people from old magazines or newspapers. Paraphrased Scripture is written in "thought balloons" and glued onto the pictures. Pictures are mounted on heavy paper and hung on the wall of the classroom.

Getting Started

Sample teacher instructions for using Picture Captions in a Conclusion activity:

"We have studied several very neat aspects of Christianity and paraphrased Scriptures which describe these aspects. Pick the statement which describes how you feel. Print it on this strip of paper with the Scripture reference. Mount it with your picture on the heavy paper I've given you."

Sharing Bible Learning

"This has been a fun project. I think we all enjoyed seeing each other's baby pictures!" This project has also reinforced the ideas expressed in these Scriptures. Let's hang our Picture Captions on the wall as a reminder of what we've learned today."

SENIOR'S GAME TIME

Purpose: To help learners apply biblical principles of service and caring to their lives.

Materials
- [ ] Notepaper
- [ ] Pens or pencils
- [ ] Coffee can (may be decorated)
- [ ] Card tables and chairs
- [ ] Variety of games: dominoes, Yahtzee, Chinese checkers, bingo, etc.
- [ ] Optional—refreshments for the game time

Procedure
Before the party:
1. Learners study biblical principles of service and caring.
2. Learners plan a time, place and details for a senior game time.
3. Older people from the congregation or neighborhood are invited.
4. Class members write their name and services they would be willing to give as prizes (i.e., I will wash your windows, I will mow your lawn, I will scrub your kitchen floor) on slips of paper. The slips of paper are then put in the coffee can.
   At the party:
5. Class members host the party, getting all the seniors involved in a game.
6. Game winners get to reach into the coffee can to get a piece of paper with a name and donated service written on it. This is their prize.
   In class next Sunday class members discuss how they felt giving the party and helping the elderly.

Variations

1. Class members may hold a "slave auction." Learners are auctioned off to the church member with the highest bid. The learner must be that person's slave for a day, responsible for doing chores for them. Money collected is then given to missions or another charitable organization.
2. Senior's game time may be given at a rest home. Gifts of visits, handmade items or services are given as prizes.

Getting Started

Sample teacher instructions for using Senior Game Time in a Conclusion activity:

"We have been studying the biblical principles of service and caring. Let's read James 2:14-19 together." Class reads verses. "Sometimes there are people right under our noses who have needs. I am thinking particularly of the older people in our own church. Let's discuss ideas of how we might be able to serve them. I have an idea which I think would help them and be a lot of fun, also. Tell me if you're interested."

Sharing Bible Learning

"We have practiced serving and caring for others by having a Senior Game Time. Let's share our reaction to the game time and also to performing our service prizes. What were some of your good experiences? Were there any unpleasant experiences? Was anything different than you expected it would be?"

MISCELLANEOUS

IF THE SHOE FITS

Purpose: To focus learners' attention on a Bible theme or personality trait of a Bible character.

Materials
☐ Bible for each learner
☐ Boxes for shoes
☐ Various shoes, sandals, boots (or magazine pictures of shoes)
☐ Paper
☐ Pencils
☐ Index cards

Procedure
1. Prior to class time locate shoes that may suggest a topic that you will be studying. (You can find many old, unusual shoes at thrift shops.) Write clear instructions on an index card. Seal a shoe (or magazine picture of a shoe) and the instructions in a box. Prepare one box for each group of three to six learners.
2. Guide learners in forming groups of three to six.
3. Each group of learners selects (or is assigned) a box. They are to discover in the Scripture being studied a person whose foot the shoe would fit. Option: The shoe may represent a person in contemporary life to whom the biblical truth being studied applies.
4. Learners work individually or as a group to write a description of the person the shoe fits. The index card from the shoe box may give additional instructions (or questions to be answered).
5. Learners share their written reports.

Variations
1. Instead of using a shoe, substitute any article that might suggest the individual (or trait) to be studied.
2. Have students create archaeological reports based on an artifact that they have found and what it suggests about the life of the person studied. Use Scripture as a reference source.

Example
   In a study of 1 Corinthians 12:12-31 shoes which represent a variety of people could be put in the boxes with instructions to the students in the group to describe how the members of their class could encourage, minister to and help the other members of the Body of Christ. Each group could describe the kind of person who might wear the shoe and give ideas of ways to be closer to and more supportive of that person.

Getting Started
   Sample teacher instructions for using If the Shoe Fits in a Bible Exploration activity:
   "As we continue our study of 1 Corinthians I would like you to do something

unusual. In each of the boxes I have given to you is a shoe and a set of instructions. I would like you to read the passage listed on your instruction sheet, decide what kind of person in our church might wear this shoe and write several paragraphs describing what students your age could do to encourage the shoe wearer. Be prepared to share your ideas with the class."

Sharing Bible Learning

"You have very good ideas for ministering to other members of the church. Let's take our lesson one step further by each selecting one of the ideas and putting it into practice this week."

MISCELLANEOUS

ROAD OF LIFE

Purpose: To help learners see God's hand in their lives.

Materials
☐ Paper
☐ Pens
☐ Optional: Colored felt pens

Procedure
1. Before class make a sample Road of Life map. This map may be purely fictitious or it may illustrate your own life.
2. Guide a class discussion of the various highs and lows learners may have experienced in their spiritual lives.
3. Show sample road map. Explain project.
4. Students create road maps of their own spiritual lives which show high points, low points, and places of importance and decision.
5. Learners share their road maps.

Variations
1. Learners may create Road of Life maps for various Bible characters being studied.
2. Learners may focus on the last six months of their lives and create a road map to illustrate this period.

Example

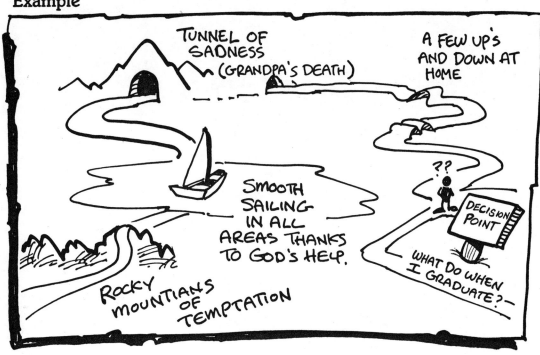

Getting Started

Sample teacher instructions for using Road of Life as an Approach activity:

"Let's take a few minutes to talk about the important events in our lives as Christians. We're going to use this information to make a road map which illustrates our life's journey so far. I've made a sample road map of my life for you to use as an example."

Sharing Bible Learning

"It is interesting to see how the Lord has worked in our lives. Some of us were born into Christian families and have had rather smooth trails. Others have met difficulties along the way and have had rocky roads. But one thing we can be sure of is that God loves us all. This was very clearly shown by Jesus when he met a man named Zacchaeus. Let's open our Bibles to Luke 19:1."